AT THE WALL :
THE 69TH PENNSYLVANIA AT GETTYSBURG

AT THE WALL :
THE 69TH PENNSYLVANIA
AT GETTYSBURG

Don Ernsberger

To order additional copies of this book, contact:
Xlibris Corporation
1-888-795-4274
www.Xlibris.com
Orders@Xlibris.com
36466

CONTENTS

DEDICATION

This book is dedicated to the reenactors who portray the 69th Pennsylvania "Irish Volunteers" in living history events, parades, school presentations and battle recreations. Their musical activities contribute to battlefield preservation and finance gravestones on the final resting places of the original 69th veterans. For the past two decades, over 200 individuals have worn the uniform, carried the rifle and placed green boxwood in their caps to recreate the spirit and actions of the original "Irish Volunteers" . Each year in November, they gather in Gettysburg to honor the lads who fought and died there.

FORWARD

This work is an edited and improved abstraction from my Two Volume regimental History "Paddy Owen's Regular's: A History of the 69th Pennsylvania "Irish Volunteers" (Xlibris publishing—Random House).

I have created the work to provide the reader with a focus on the Battle of Gettysburg and give, what I believe, is the most detailed examination of the hand to hand fighting at the wall on July 3, 1863 ever produced.

I give a special thanks to my life long friend David Walter who helped with editing and provided ideas on improvement. Dave, who is working on an upcoming Civil War novel, has been a long time Civil War buff and is active in Brandywine Civil War Roundtable in Chester County Pennsylvania.

The reader will note several extended footnote segments which provide my personal analysis of a number of ever—debated tactical issues about the Battle of Gettysburg such as the actions of the 59th New York infantry and the location of the companies of the 71st Pennsylvania Infantry. I have attempted to provide evidence using official records; pension files and logic.

The reader will also noted that I have not changed the spelling in the personal letters cited in this work. I wanted the reader to have the full flavor of the language used in communicating with loved ones at home.

Finally, I would offer the reader a sample of the other Civil War products I have produced. In addition to this work and my Two Volume study Paddy Owen's Regular's, I also have published two computer CD studies of tactical history on Pickett's Charge at Gettysburg July 3, 1863 and the Second Corps assault on the "Mule Shoe" at Spotsylvania May 12, 1864. These CD's provide a narrated minute by minute series of maps of the action on the regimental level of each attack. They each include diary entries, background charts and explanation of action.

Feel free to use my website for full details *www.Pa69irish.com*

CHAPTER ONE

BACKGROUND

The core of the officers and men who would form the 69th Pennsylvania "Irish Volunteers" came from roots reaching back to the local Philadelphia Irish neighborhood militia units. The Irish militias been formed in conjunction with the local Democratic party in the city which had a need for political and military strength that would be loyal to the Democrats in times of civil strife. In addition many in the Irish community saw the militias as a way to advance Irish Nationalism and to promote and protect Irish culture. Others recalled the anti-Irish riots of the 1840's and saw a need for a neighborhood militia to protect Irish immigrant homes and churches from the nativist violence which had occurred throughout the period of intense Irish immigration after the potato famines of the 1840's. These local militias were often named after Irish-American heroes had names such as The Meagher Guards, The Hibernian Greens, The Shields Guards, The Jackson Artillery and the Emmett Guards. Men active in these militia companies who would latter rise as officers of the 69th Pa included James Harvey, Dennis O'Kane, James Duffy and George Thompson. Each company practiced marching, drill and firearms use, and each maintained a local arsenal. It was natural, therefore, that when President Abraham Lincoln called for the states to provide volunteer regiments to put down the rebellion in April 1861, that local militias would be called for such service. However, many political leaders showed little interest in the use of Irish militia units and preferred more traditional regiments of Anglo-Saxon makeup. Anti-Irish feelings still ran strong in Pennsylvania. Finally on May 8, 1861 a variety of local Irish militia companies were merged together to form the 24th Pa three month volunteers. But these Irishmen were not to have one of their own as a commander. Instead an active Democratic politician and lawyer named Joshua Owen was named as Colonel with Dennis O'Kane, who had been a leader in the Irish militia community as Lieutenant Colonel. Owen, a Welshman, would provide the political link with the largely Democratic Irish community and avoid having an Irishman as Colonel.

The 24th Pa trained and then marched off to the Harper's Ferry region and served under General Robert Patterson's command. Patterson was himself an Irishman who had been born in County Tyrone. The soldiers correspondence of the period is filled with references to the lack of supplies, arms and payment that many of the regiment felt was linked to anti-Irish Catholic feelings. During their service, the men of the 24th never did receive new uniforms and were issued food and supplies infrequently. They were issued inferior weapons as well. One soldier, Michael Burk was severely injured when a gun exploded in his hands during firing practice. Quickly, Colonel Joshua Owen became close to his men, fighting for their interests. In fact, the derisive label "Paddy Owen" was embraced by the colonel as his chosen nickname. About the time of the expiration of their 3 month term the Battle of First Bull Run occurred and, while the plea for a short term extension of service was denied by many regiments in Harper's Ferry, the 24th Pa agreed to stay in the field for an additional two weeks.

Upon their return to Philadelphia, a series of meetings occurred among the leaders of the 24th with regard to reenlisting the unit in the war effort. Many expressed the views that their treatment in the past three months warranted no reenlistment. Some vowed to go to New York and join Brigadier Thomas Meagher's famous Irish 69th NY infantry. Others thought of demanding an Irish Colonel as a precondition to service. The issue remained, of course, whether the Pennsylvania government would welcome an Irish three year regiment. On a regimental fund raising excursion for war orphans to Atlantic City New Jersey discussions began in earnest.

The arrival of Senator Edward Baker of Oregon in Philadelphia in July of 1861 provided an opportunity. Baker had attempted to recruit a Union brigade in California, where he had practiced law for ten years but was unable. His good friend President Abraham Lincoln authorized him to recruit in the east and he soon was in New York City and in Philadelphia raising his "California" brigade. While traveling through Philadelphia he met with "Paddy" Owen and some of the former 24th Pa officers and offered immediate pay, federal pensions and fair treatment to the former 24th Pa under the banner of the "California Brigade". Owen was able to convince many Irish veterans to join the new regiment that would be nicknamed the "2nd California". Soon

Joshua Owen—First Colonel of the regiment

10 companies were formed and trained at Owen's Chestnut Hill estate and the men were off to Washington DC. on September 17. Upon arrival they marched to Chain Bridge, Virginia on the Potomac River and began to help complete Fort Ethan Allen. Their departure from Philadelphia was far from a positive send off to heroes as many Philadelphians greeted their march to the trains with catcalls and thrown objects.

After several months at Fort Ethan Allen the "California Brigade" was moved to winter quarters in Poolesville Maryland and assigned the task of guarding Potomac River crossing points. Here the Battle of Ball's Bluff occurred on October 21, 1861 where Colonel Edward Baker was killed. Baker became the only sitting US Senator killed in battle. The 69th (2nd California) was in reserve at that battle. A series of political maneuvers then resulted in the regiments of the "California Brigade" being shifted to Pennsylvania Volunteer status with the "Irish" being renamed first the 68th Pa (for a short time) and finally the 69th Pa. The newly constituted "Philadelphia Brigade" brigade came under the command of General William Burns and was involved in an expedition to the Shenandoah Valley in Virginia. Here on February 22, 1862 the regiment was presented with its first green battle flag a gift of Irish citizens of Philadelphia.

After the winter of 1861-1862 ended, plans began for General George McClellan's Peninsular campaign to Richmond. "Paddy Owen's Regulars" would be in the midst of the battles that occurred from Yorktown to Grapevine bridge and then Fair Oaks. The regiment became a part of the 2nd Brigade, 2nd Division 2nd Corps under Brigadier John Sedgwick. At Yorktown the regiment suffered it's first battle death to explosive "torpedoes" buried in the dirt by retreating rebels. As the Army of the Potomac retreated toward the James River after Robert E lee launched a flank offensive the 69th was in the rear guard at Peach Orchard and at Savage Station. At Savage Station they were ordered to flank the advance of the famous confederate ironclad railcar and turned it back.

The next day at the Battle of Glendale, the regiment earned distinction when they launched (in the words of General Sedgwick) "The first successful bayonet charge of the war," helping to recapture a Union artillery battery. In the June 1862 retreat, the unit had suffered 10 killed and 32 wounded plus a loss of 5 prisoners in several battles before settling into camp at Harrison's Landing on the James river.

The 69th was next rushed back to Washington in late August toaid in the defense against Lee's advance, after the defeat of Pope's army at Second Bull Run, participating in action near Centerville, Va. Soon they were marching west toward Antietam Creek. At the battle of Antietam, Maryland on September 17th, 1862, the 69th along with the other regiments of the Philadelphia Brigade (71st, 72nd and 106th) participated in the ill fated advance by Sedgwick's division against the West Woods. That advance walked into a trap and was attacked on three sides and driven back. The 69th lost 21 killed and 57 wounded as well as 10 captured in the fighting. After Antietam, the regiment reentered Virginia in pursuit of Confederate forces.

McClellan's replacement by General Ambrose Burnside also saw Joshua Owen advance to the position of Brigade commander as Brigadier General, and Dennis O'Kane was promoted to Colonel of the regiment. The "Irish Volunteers" now had an Irish commander. Burnside took the regiment to Fredericksburg where it participated in the assault on Marye's Heights. In that failed assault, the 69th was pinned down for several hours on the slopes and had heavy casualties numbering 19 killed, 32 wounded and 8 captured.

Dennis O'Kane—First Lieutenant Colonel of the Regiment

During the Chancellorsville campaign the "Philadelphia Brigade" was given a duty to cover Rappahannock river crossings that would be used either to rush reinforcements to Sedgwick's Fredericksburg wing or to aid in his withdrawal. As Sedgwick withdrew the 69th covered that retreat and destroyed the pontoon bridges behind them. The rest of May and most of June of 1863 was spent in camp near Fredericksburg, Virginia facing the confederate forces. The first two years had cost the regiment many of the older men from the Irish militia days but new lads rose to officer status. Several officers had resigned from the regiment due to political differences with Colonel O'Kane.

On June 14th, the 69th was alerted to rush north toward Pennsylvania as Lee invaded their home state. Setting mileage records as they marched, the regiment was about to participate in the Gettysburg campaign. Here they would find their "finest hours".

CHAPTER TWO

THE MARCH TO GETTYSBURG

As May 1863 drew to a close, rumors were flying about Confederate troop movements that might well mark a new offensive operation by Lee. Changes in Confederate picket activity and movements of rebel camp locations seemed to signal that something was stirring. The brigade historian, Charles Banes, wrote "Troops could be seen changing their locations, and new camps appeared on the south side of Fredericksburg. The pickets of the enemy became more bold and insolent, evidently exhibiting the feeling of confidence imparted to their entire army by the battles of Fredericksburg and Chancellorsville." 1

One false alarm had occurred on the last day of May when a large group of Confederate troops were observed fishing and washing clothes in the Rappahannock River across from the Philadelphia Brigade skirmish line. The report of this gathering prompted the entire Brigade to be placed in battle positions for a short time until the situation was evaluated. 2

On June 1, the 69th was paid up to April 1, and the muster rolls that day gave a picture of the regimental strengths. A total of 389 men were present and accounted for on May 30 in Falmouth, Va. Of these, 52 were sick and injured in field hospitals and would not march north with the regiment.

A company by company look at the muster rolls shows just how hard the rigors of campaigning had depleted the 69th. These findings were typical of any regiment in the Union army. From company A, under Captain McHugh (2nd), Sergeant Martin Healy had been granted a furlough to return to Philadelphia on March 15th and had chosen to desert the regiment on May 5th. The 26-year-old former dyer born in Queens County, Ireland had fought in all the battles up to Fredericksburg but would never return. Private Daniel

Crowley in the same company had been sick during the month of May and was sent to a Washington DC hospital. He would miss Gettysburg but return to the regiment in August. He would become sick again in September, be sent to a Philadelphia hospital and released Dec 1, 1863. That very night he fell through a bridge in Philadelphia and was killed. The third man in company A who would not be marching north was Private John Curtin, who had gotten sick in November 1862, and had sent to a hospital in Washington DC. In August, the 29-year-old Queens County, Ireland born shoemaker would be transferred to the invalid corps but recovered enough by February 1864 to return to the regiment. Private Arthur Carroll, in company A, was also sick in a Washington, DC hospital and Private Robert Griffith was on detached duty in West Chester, Pa

Company B was down seven men plus was missing their Captain John McHugh. McHugh (not related to Captain John McHugh 2nd from company A) was on furlough in Philadelphia and would not return until after Gettysburg. He had been had been shot in the knee by accidental discharge of a pistol. In fact, he would become AWOL after July 10th leading to a Court-Martial. Private Charles Bettinger had deserted on May 6th from camp at Falmouth. The 35-year-old former carpenter, who had only joined the regiment April 10, 1863, would never return. Sergeant Thomas Reardon would be granted a furlough to visit Philadelphia in May and, instead of returning to camp for the march north, the 23 year old sailor from Boston would desert in Philadelphia on June 6th. Reardon had fought bravely in all the engagements in the war up to that time. Among the sick in hospitals were Private John Keelin, Charles McCullough, Matthew McNamara, Roger Laughlin and Thomas Hanlon. Keelin had joined the regiment in August 1861 and had been sick once before in early 1862. On May 10 the Monahan born laborer took sick and would miss the Gettysburg campaign. He would be discharged January 17th, 1864 due to heart problems. McCullough had been born in Tyrone, Ireland and was 29 years old. He had been a tailor before the war and had been sick since April 23. Laughlin, who had been wounded at Antietam at age 39, had contracted a case of inflammation of the testicles (Orchetis) and had entered the Potomac Creek Hospital on April 17th. Loughlin had immigrated to America from Killeshill Parish, Dungannon District, County Tyrone with his father and brother, John and sister, Ann. He had married Bridget McMahon before the war. She died in 1863 while he was hospitalized. Thomas Hanlon, age 40 entered the same hospital on April 27th with serious diarrhea and was transferred first to Washington DC hospitals and then to

Philadelphia. He was discharged from the army in September 1864. Private Hugh McCall had been detailed to Corps headquarters service.

Company C had gone through some changes. Captain James O'Reilly and 1st Lieutenant John Connor had both resigned their commissions in April, and with Lieutenant Hugh Flood gone from his Fredericksburg wounds, Charles Fitzpatrick and Michael Dougherty—both who had been wounded at Glendale—were promoted to command the company. The company would be missing five more men. Private James Campbell had been sick at Harper's Ferry back in October 1862 and had transferred from hospital to hospital until dismissed in March 1863. The Tyrone-born Campbell was 34 years old when he left the service. His brother, Samuel, apparently deserted around the same date. Another Campbell, William, had been badly wounded at Fredericksburg and remained in a hospital. (Only John Campbell would remain to fight at Gettysburg). Two men from the company had been detached: Private Thomas McQuillan, age 41 who had been wounded at Fredericksburg to Philadelphia hospital duty, and Private William Gallagher, age 36, who had been sick at Harper's Ferry had remained on hospital duty since October 1862.

Captain Tinen's company D was down ten men. Private John F Boyle (one of the two John Boyles in the company) had taken sick in October and would linger sick in Washington DC until October when he was discharged. At 45, he had been born in Ireland and worked as a laborer in Philadelphia before the war. Also in Company D, at the start of the war, had been Corporal William Smith from Danville, Pa. He had taken ill in September 1862 before Antietam and was in a York, Pa hospital where he remained until he deserted on April 18, 1864. Another man absent hospitalized was Private Dennis Leary from Danville, Pa who had joined the 69th along with his two friends William Paugh and Patrick Connolly who worked with him in the Iron Mill in Danville. Leary, a native of Cork had only been in the United States eight months before joining the army. In March, 1863 he had developed rheumatism of the ankle and was hospitalized and, by December, would be transferred to the Reserve Corps. Leary's friend Paugh was hospitalized April 16, 1863 and never truly recovered until the war was over. Private Michael Sex had been in hospitals since the third month of the war with an eye disease and would not return to the regiment until April 1864 when he was hospitalized again two weeks later with a leg ulcer caused by a piece of ice. Two men still were recovering from wounds. Private Terrance O'Neill, wounded at Fredericksburg was still hospitalized and Private Michael Roach had been discharged after being hospitalized with Antietam wounds.

Company E, which was commanded by 1st Lieutenant Thomas Wood after the murder of Captain Andrew McManus, was missing eight men. McManus had been shot to death by an officer of the 71st Pennsylvania in a personal dispute back in May. Private William Collins, the 16 year old company drummer had been sick in the hospital for the past two months and would be transferred to the Invalid Corps after Gettysburg. Private Martin Reilly had been suffering with eye problems ever since the end of the Peninsular campaign. He had fought at Antietam and Fredericksburg but was bothered by ulcers in his eyes. Finally, on May 20, Surgeon Burmeister placed the 35 year-old Roscommon, Ireland native in a Washington hospital. His eyes were operated upon unsuccessfully. He would remain in the hospital until April 9th 1864 when he was discharged. One man in company E who would have missed his pay on May 30th was Private Dennis Hughes, who had left camp and deserted the day before. There were two men named Mooney in Company E. They were not related, but both missed the Gettysburg campaign due to wounds they had each received at Fredericksburg. Private Thomas Mooney had been born in Donegal and had been a 27-year-old laborer before joining the 69th. He was wounded in the attack on Fredericksburg heights by a minie ball in the arm and would not return to his company until February 1864. Private James Mooney was also hit at Fredericksburg (right hip and abdomen) and was still recovering in Philadelphia. Private James Devlin was still a deserter in Philadelphia after being captured at Antietam and then parolld. He would be caught shortly after the Gettysburg battle and returned to the regiment. Two others were still under arrest in Philadelphia, Privates Daniel Mahone and Patrick Sullivan.

Two men in company F would not march north under Captain Thompson due to desertion. Private Andrew Hughes had been wounded in the Antietam fighting and was supposed to be in a Philadelphia hospital, Word reached the 69th regiment that the 26-year-old former painter had deserted in Philadelphia on May 21, never to return. Private William Seary had been wounded in the face at Fredericksburg and was in a Philadelphia hospital. Like Hughes, he too, would desert. On May 21st the 19-year-old former baker walked out of the hospital and never returned to the 69th Pa. Private James Kelly was sick in Potomac Creek hospital and would later be transferred to the Invalid Corps in the Fall of 1863. Kelly had begun as a 35 year old Corporal but was demoted in November 8, 2003 at Camp Observation.

Company G, with Captain Hugh Boyle in command, would be missing one soldier. Corporal Thomas Jordan, who had been hurt by fragments at Malvern Hill, back in July 1862 took sick on May 2nd and would remain in the hospital until September. The 28-year-old married man would return and be promoted to Sergeant in the fall. Captain Boyle was not in great condition. His wound from Antietam had still not healed well and he was troubled by abscesses on his leg. He would travel to Gettysburg but be too sick to fight at the head of his company. Seven men from Company G had been detached to ambulance or teamster duty.

Captain Thomas Kelly, Company H, would be on detached service taking care of Quartermaster duties after June 5th, and Bernard Sherry would command the company during the March north and the fighting at Gettysburg. Sherry's command would be missing three men. Private James Hamilton had taken sick at Harper's Ferry in October 1862 and on May would be discharged from the hospital and leave the service. Private James McHenry, who had joined company H in September 1862, became sick by April 24 1863 at Aquia Landing hospital and would be discharged as his company was already on their way north. Sergeant James Barr had been a teamster before the war and was detached to service in Philadelphia. He deserted his duty there, around the time of the Gettysburg campaign but later returned to serve.

Michael Duffy's company I had four men whom would miss the march north. Private James Brannigin had joined the regiment in August 1861, but by October 1862 had deserted at Harper's Ferry but was caught and returned. He became sick and was placed in a Baltimore hospital in March where he remained while the Battle of Gettysburg raged. He deserted from here on July 18th 1863 only to be caught again and serve until killed at Cold Harbor. Today, he lies in Arlington National Cemetery, one of five members of the 69th Pa to rest there. Another company "I" soldier, sick in a hospital at that time, was Private Alfred Hill who had taken sick at Fort Monroe back in August 1862 and remained in hospitals until the end of the 1863 when he deserted and disappeared. Finally William White's 22 year old friend Sylvester Campbell, who had taken sick at Harper's Ferry, was still ill in an Alexandria Hospital and would be transferred to the Invalid Corps. Private Robert Goss who had been wounded back at the first action at Munson Hill still remained hospitalized in Philadelphia.

Sickness and desertion had cost Captain William Davis and company K four men before the march north began. Private Patrick Fox was given a furlough home in mid-April and would desert May 16th. The 37-year-old former cordwainer, born in Clendragh, Ireland, fought in the Battle of Glendale but had been sick for much of the war. Private Davis Bruce took ill and was sent to Fort Monroe back in August 16, 1862. He returned to duty for the Battle of Fredericksburg but took sick again May 2 and was sent to Washington DC for care. By September he would recover and rejoin the company. The 29-year-old photographer would stay with the unit until the end of the war. Private Charles Donnelly, who was a 19-year-old former cotton spinner from the mills of Philadelphia, left camp on May 30th and deserted. He had been active in all battle and skirmishes up to that time but would never again fight with the 69th. The last of the four from Company K was Private John Robinson who had deserted back in October 1862 and was arrested and returned. His behavior in camp led to a court martial, and he would be sent to prison until the end of the war.

In addition a number of detachments were made within the regiment. The carnage of Fredericksburg had shown that there was a need for more personnel in the medical staff. To strengthen this branch Privates Michael Walsh from company C, and Henry Owens, from Company E, were detached. Private Walsh was detached from company C to work in the hospital with the Second Corps ambulance detachment. He was a 36 year old soldier from Philadelphia and, while caring for the wounded after Gettysburg, contracted Typhoid fever and died in Philadelphia October 1, 1863 at the South Street Hospital. Private Owens was 21 years old and had served with the infantry in all it's battles. He would be detached as a Corps ambulance driver corps. Later in the war, he would be captured while on ambulance service. The fourth transfer to the Corps ambulance unit would be Private Patrick McGlinchy. He was a 40 year old native of Donegal, Ireland who would, in 1864, shift to nurse duty with the Division hospital.

June 2 brought fine weather and a Division Drill conducted by General John Gibbon on the fields outside camp. Gibbon had risen to command the 2nd Division of the 2nd Corps after distinguished service in the war. Gibbon, had formed strong negative opinions about Brigadier General Joshua Owen which would soon surface. Perhaps he disliked the level of discipline Owen had shown in his Brigade. Perhaps it was the fact that Owen was a political appointment and not a West Point product. This day saw the desertion from the regiment of Private James Reynolds, Company C. The 29 year old Tipperary, Ireland born soldier had been a printer before the war and had joined in August 1861. He would never be caught. Sometime during that day Corporal William Smith in company D left camp.

The following day, June 3, on the north side of the Rappahannock river, General Owen held a brigade dress parade and drill (perhaps to sharpen up the soldiers from their performance the day before for Gibbon). Meanwhile unknown to the Union army, on the south side of the Rappahannock the Confederate divisions of General John Bell Hood and General Lafayette McLaws of Lieutenant General James Longstreet's Corps began moving away from Fredericksburg heading west then north.

During the day, Colonel O'Kane wrote a letter to Pennsylvania Albert Governor Curtin informing him about promotions he had made within the regiment . . . .

Camp near Falmouth, Va.
June 3, 1863

His Excellency A.G. Curtin
Governor Penna

Governor,
    I have the honor to transmit the annexed list of promotions in my regiment with the request that commissions may be forwarded at as early a day possible. The 2nd Lieutenant of Company A (James Cole) is now under arrest & I have not therefore promoted him. Patrick Healy, whom the Governor desired promoted if possible, died in March last. Murdock Campbell of Company B you will perceive has been promoted

Very Respectfully
Your obt. Servant
D. O'Kane
Col. Commanding Regt. 3

An incident marred the night of June 3rd. In camp, Corporal Robert Morrison in company A, formerly of Company M, had been drinking and was told by his Captain to return to his quarters and to be quiet. Morrison refused and was taken to the guardhouse by a sentry. Once there, he began berating his Captain, John McHugh, charging that McHugh had purchased his commission for $1000 and that he, Morrison, was just as good a man as McHugh but lacked money to buy a commission. Morrison then threatened

McHugh's life by stating "McHugh's brother was killed at Antietam and perhaps Morrison might have a load for the Captain some day." The incident was witnessed by Sergeant Ralph Rickaby, Corporal Patrick Moran, and Sergeant of the Guard Hugh Kelly and Corporal Dennis McGowen. Morrison had been demoted from Sergeant to Private back in December 1861. Morrison was Court Martialed, demoted to Private again and scheduled for punishment after the Gettysburg Campaign was complete. The married father of a one-year-old son would be killed one month later at the wall in Gettysburg.

That same evening (June 3) Captain Thomas Kelly (Co H) wrote a letter on behalf of his brother Charles concerning the amount of time that had passed since Charles' received a brevet commission as 2nd Lieutenant . . . .

Headquarters 69th Regt. PV Vol
Camp Near Falmouth, Va.
June 4, 1863
Major G.W. Bardwell

Sir;

My brother Charles F Kelly has been recommended by Col. O'Kane to the Governor for commission as 2nd Lieut. of Company H (vice Sheridan dismissed) of which Company he is now first Sergt.

He cannot be mustered out as Sergt and in as a Lieut. unless he has the commission in his possession and as the 30th of June is Muster day it is necessary that he will lose one month's pay and the date of muster will be one month later than it should be. Knowing the delays that take place in regard to the forwarding of Commissions to officers unless they are attended to personally by some friend I have taken the Liberty of asking that favour of you. If you can and will facilitate the forwarding of his commission to him you will place me under lasting obligations. Hoping this will find you in the enjoyment of good health.

I remain Respectfully
Your Most Obedient
Thomas Kelly
captain Comp H 69th Regt Pa Vol
Acting Regt Quartermaster
to Major G.W. Bardwell
Harrisburg 4

On June 5th Colonel O'Kane made public his changes in command in General Orders No. 14 . . . .

Headquarters 69th Regt P.V.
Camp near Falmouth, Va. June 5, 1863
General Orders
No 14

The following appointments are made to fill vacancies and the appointees respectfully recommended to the Governor of Penna for confirming Commission to date from this day.

1st Lieut. John McHugh, Co A to be Captain Co. A in place of Capt. Duffy promoted to Major March 31, 1863.

2nd Lieut. John McIlvane to be 1st Lieutenant of Co. B in place of 1st Lieut. Michael Cassidy dismissed May 20, 1863.

Sergt. Major Murdock Campbell (late 1st Sgt. Co B) to be 2nd Lieut. Co B in place of Lieutenant McIlvan promoted.

1st Lieut Thomas Woods of Co. E to be Capt. of Co E in place of Capt. Andrew McManus deceased.

2nd Lieut John J Devlin of Co E to be 1st Lieut. of Co. E in place of Lieutenant Woods promoted.

1st Sergt John Taggert of Co E to be 2nd Lieut. of Co E in place of Lieutenant Devlin promoted.

1st Lieut. Hugh Boyle of Co. G to be Capt. of Co G in place of Capt Moran resigned and discharged Feb 21, 1863

2nd Lieut. Bernard Sherry of Co G to be 1st Lieut. of Co G Lieutenant Boyle promoted. 5

While O'Kane and his men engaged in the soldier's age-old promotions game, at Army central command, that night, the commanding General Joseph General Hooker was nervous and decided to send out some infantry and Calvary units to see what Lee was doing. He would move Infantry across the Rappahannock River at Fredericksburg and send cavalry patrols west across the Rappahannock at Kelly's and Beverly Fords.

In the midst of these developments the attention of the men of the 69th was focused in their own camp and on the Court Martial Trial of Captain Bernard McMahon of the 71st Pa for the murder on May 27th of Captain

Andrew McManus of the 69th's company E. The levels of emotion and calls for revenge had still not waned. McManus had been a man loved by almost all of the 69th regiment for he had been in the nucleus of the "Irish Volunteers" since before the war as a member of the "Meagher Guards". He had been captain of Company K of the 24thPa and had led Company E of the 69th since the beginning of the war. When the court martial of McMahon began at 11:00 in the morning of June 5th the full attention of the 69th regiment was on the proceedings. McMahon would be found guilt and sentence to be shot.

The next morning the sounds of artillery could be heard off to the east as a massive cannonade preceded the crossing of the Rappahannock River by two divisions of Sedgwick' Sixth Corps. Their mission was to cross the river at the point where General William B. Franklin had crossed back in December and test the rebel defense there. The mission ran into strong rebel opposition and it seemed to Union leadership that Lee was still entrenched after all. It turned out that the spot picked for the crossing was one of the few spots still strongly entrenched by the Confederates. The next day, June 7th, the Second Corps was told to be prepared to pack up camp and move. Wagonmaster Jacob Rittenhouse was told to pack up all supplies and be ready to load tents. Commissary Sergeant Hugh Logan was ordered to prepare three days rations for the men's haversacks.

This news unnerved at least one soldier, sometime that evening Private Thomas Reardon in company B from Boston, Massachusetts left camp and deserted. The 23 year old former sailor was never heard from again. For the next several days, the regiment waited in camp, ate all the rations they had prepared, unloaded wagons and pondered their next move. On June 9th, The Second Corps commander, Major General Darius Couch who had requested a transfer due to animosity toward General Hooker was relieved of command and replaced by Major General Winfield Scott Hancock a native of Norristown Pa. On June 10th Lieutenant James Cole of Company A officially left the army as a result of his Court-Marital for "conduct unbecoming an officer". He would travel back to Philadelphia as his regiment prepared to travel north after Robert E Lee. The same day Private Roger Coyle deserted camp.

Sometime, after being paid, Private John Boyle in Company I would take time before breaking camp to have a photograph taken to be sent to a female friend named Sallie back in Philadelphia. he sent it home with Captain Tinens wife who was returning to Philadelphia. he enclosed the following letter to his mother with instructions. The likeness would no doubt become a cherished item as Private Boyle would die at Gettysburg in less than a month . . . .

> Dear Mother
>   I send by Mrs. Tinen my likeness to Sallie. I have directed it to your care and wish yu would give it to Ellen and she can deliver it privately. I am waiting for a letter from you everyday. I sent $30 home yesterday Adams Express.
>
> I remain Your Affectionate Son
J.C. Boyle

Lee's vanguard, commanded by Lieutenant General Richard Ewell, had already advanced north, nearly as far as Winchester, Virginia and Union cavalry patrols were still uncertain as to the intention of Lee's Army. Finally on the 11th of June, the troops were give orders to be ready to march on June 14th and once again the wagons were packed. This time, all extra baggage and belongings would be sent to Washington, DC and food prepared for a three day march. The humid day would be spent packing baggage and disguising the camp to prevent knowledge by the rebels of their impending departure. Extra tents were pitched in sight of rebel pickets. Straw was stuffed into old uniforms and broken rifles placed on breastwork walls. The men were told to pack everything except tents, which would be put into the wagons after dark. Around 8:00PM the 69th marched out of camp, and after going only three miles, were turned around and sent back to where they started. The men slept on the damp earth that night and were told to be ready to march before dawn. Musician Peter Moore, age 24, left camp this night and was reported as a deserter the next day. The company K soldier's military record read "Has been in all the engagements with the company (excepting Fredericksburg) up to the time of desertion." He would never return.

On June 14th Private Patrick Hewitt in company A deserted the regiment as they left Falmouth, Virginia. The 27-year-old soldier, born in Limerick, had been a laborer before the war and would be captured by rebel cavalry nearby. He was sent to Richmond prison but quickly put on the Parole list to be sent to City Point, Va. on June 20th. He apparently caught Typhoid fever from other prisoners and died at the Annapolis hospital on Aug 3. One man in company I dropped out of the march the same day. Private George Melvin was missing the next morning when roll was taken by First Sergeant William Richardson. Melvin, from Tyrone, was 27 years old had been a tailor before the war and had joined the 69th Pa in January of 1863. He was assigned to company I and told a number of his new comrades that he had been a soldier prior to enlisting in the 69th. He disappeared on June 14th and was captured by Confederate partisans along the roads near Fredericksburg. He would be taken to Richmond prison and paroled at City Point, Va. on July 19th. After arriving at Camp Parole he deserted again and was not seen again in the army. His service record reads "Has never been in an engagement. To be charged with one Enfield rifle and one full set of equipment." Private James McVey, 26, became sick and dropped out of the march. He would be transferred to the Invalid Corps in September from a Washington DC hospital. McVey would recover and reenlist in the 69th on February 1, 1864 and then be killed at the Wilderness in May.

On June 14th, Confederates under Major General Jubal Early and Major General Edward Johnson attached and routed Union forces at Winchester under Union Commander Major General Milroy. The way north was wide open. At 3:00 AM June 15th, the brigade was on the march again headed toward Stafford Court House some 8 miles down the road. Wagonmaster Jacob Rittenhouse was close behind with the 22 wagons of the regimental train. When they reached Stafford Courthouse, they stopped for two hours to rest. After resting, the 69th was on the road again headed for the Aquia church. By noon, the temperatures were up to 90 degrees and the wet humid weather made the men miserable in their wool uniforms. Men started dropping out of formation from heat exhaustion. "The weather was extremely hot and oppressive, the march long and the roads very dusty, many men were obliged to fall out, being overcome by the heat." **6**

One of these men was Private James McPeak in company D. Born in the village of Derrygarve in the County Derry, Ireland, he joined the 69th in August 1861 at age 29. McPeak would collapse with exhaustion June 15 and be sent to Camp Convalescent, Virginia until he recovered enough to be transferred to the Veterans Corps in September. After the war, he would return to his village in Ireland die and be buried there. Back in April Corporal Isaac Van Zant had been detached as Hospital warden. His job was to keep track of the flow of men to the medical staff and to be sure things were orderly in the medical hospital area. Van Zant was born in Bucks County Pa and was one of the 69th's few Quakers. His administrative skills would find him serving as Acting Regimental Quartermaster after Hugh Logan damaged his leg June 28th. The regiment stopped 18 miles north of their stating point short of Dunfries, VA and just past the Quantico creek. Another man who collapsed with exhaustion was Private Dennis Murray in Company D. Murray, who joined in August 1861, had deserted the regiment at Yorktown on the march back to Newport News from Harrison's Landing. He had returned by October 1862. Murray would be sent to a hospital and then transferred to the Invalid Corps. The men enjoyed the cold water of the creek as they passed and made camp in the late afternoon. The men realized that they had not experienced this kind of marching since last their march to Falmouth in November. That night Private John Frazier, in company I, left camp and deserted. Born in Inverness Scotland, Frazier, age 28, had just joined the 69th in January 1863. His captain, Michael Duffy, wrote of him "As a soldier this man is worthless, has never been in an engagement". 7

The leadership of the Regiment—Owen—O'Kane—Tschudy

The men slept through the evening and were awakened at 2:30AM June 16th to continue the march to Dunfries. Commissary Sergeant Logan and Privates Flood, Sossaman and Prenderville prepared another three days rations for the lads when the regiment took a break upon reaching Dunfries. By 4:00, the 69th reached the Steele farm at Wolf Run Shoals 10 miles north near Woodbridge and made camp for the night. During the march that day, Sergeant James White of Company A fainted and was taken to the Queen Street hospital in Alexandria, Va. The 42-year-old soldier from Philadelphia would recover and be placed in the Reserve Corps a few months later. From Company E, Private John Meade, age 35 from Roscommon, Ireland took sick and found his way to the Corps hospital. One of the original recruits of Captain Frost in Company M, Meade would be sent back to Washington DC and hospitalized in Alexandria. On October 9th he would desert from the hospital, be arrested and then take sick again and be discharged.

The brigade was permitted to sleep late on June 17th and by 8:00AM was on the road inland toward Fairfax, VA. The hike in the heat caused additional men to drop out with heat exhaustion. Private William Rourke in company C developed pains in his back and headaches. He collapsed and was taken to the Fairfax Seminary several days later. Rourke had been wounded at Fredericksburg in his left arm and the top of his head. He would be returned to his company August 24, 1863. Private John Kerns from Company K took sick and was hospitalized during the day. Kerns would not return to the regiment until the winter of 1863-1864 and would be killed at Jerusalem Plank Road in June 1864.

When the brigade reached the Sangers Station on the Orange and Alexandria Railroad, it stopped and made camp beside the Centreville road. June 18th was a day of rest. During the afternoon a thunderstorm blew down some tents but brought cool refreshing rainwater to the dirty and tired lads. Private Michael Roach became sick and was sent to a Washington DC hospital. This 27-year-old soldier, who had been wounded at Antietam, was diagnosed with Tuberculosis and dismissed from the service.

During this day of rest a number of soldiers reported to the medical staff and were diagnosed as being too sick to continue the march. Three Privates from Company G were all too sick to continue the march North. Private Patrick Garvin, who would later be killed at the Wilderness, was bothered with nausea, rapid heartbeat and pains for the past several days and, at age 33, was sent to Fairfax Seminary for rest. His doctor there stated on his report "Has been complaining for the past three weeks but did not give up until three days ago." 8 Private Francis McLaughlin, in the same company, was

too sick to travel as well. He was also sent to a hospital for rest. Alexander
Collins, the third Private in Co G to collapse on the road the day before, was
also dismissed from the march. Collins, age 26 had been slightly wounded at
Antietam and had been sickly ever since that date. He would be discharged
August 28, 1864 after a long illness.

While the regiment rested near Centreville, Private Charles Dorrington,
Company B, was arrested by the provost guard and would be sent to jail.
His military record shows that he was "apprehended as a deserter" and
fined $30 to pay for his arrest. The Dublin born Dorrington would pay off
his fines and reenlist in the regiment. Back in Philadelphia he had 5 children
to support after his wife had died before the war. He would desert two more
times before the end of the war.

At 8:00 Am on Friday June 19th the 69th was up again and heading toward
Centreville, Va. some 7 miles down the road where they camped again.
Private Patrick Leister of Company F of the 69th Pa got a chance to write
his wife a short letter on June 19th where he explained the marching and its
effects . . . .

Centerville Virginia June 19, 1863

Dear wife and Children
I take this opportunity of writing those few lines to you to let
you know that I am well after 6 hard days March but we have about
80 Miles more to go. I cant tell how manny died on the road
                                                        No More at present
                        But remain your affectiond husband Patrick Lester **9**

The morning of the 20th saw Gibbon's division headed down the
Warrenton Turnpike toward Thoroughfare Gap. The regiment crossed the
old battlefields of First and Second Bull Run and observed the remains of
horses and men that had been unearthed by wild pigs and rainstorms. The
afternoon brought a thunderstorm that turned the roads to mud. Across the
stone bridge to Gainesville and then on to Haymarket they marched. By
nightfall they were still not at their destination and so they continued in the
dark until finally they reached Thoroughfare Gap and its strategic position
Here in the dark men started falling into ditches and over large stones by the
roadside and a number of men were injured.

That same day, back in Philadelphia, the surgeon in charge of Captain John McHugh's accidental knee injury would give him another extension of his leave of absence . . . .

U.S.A. Officers Hospital, Phila June 20, 1863

> I certify that Capt. John McHugh, 69th Regt Penna Vols. Co B is a patient in this Hospital that he is suffering from a contusion of the knee received by accident. And further in my opinion, he is unfit to resume his duties, in a less period than 20 days.
>
> Wm. Camac
> Surg. In Charge
> Officers Hospital **10**

The extension of John McHugh's leaves of absence on June 20th for another 20 days would result in his missing the Gettysburg Campaign, and 1st Lieutenant McIlvane commanded the company at Gettysburg. The 69th camped beside the old mill that sat in the middle of the Gap.

However, Lee's men were already across the Potomac and entering Pennsylvania. General Jenkin's cavalry reached Chambersburg on the 15th. For the next two days the 69th would be stationed at Thoroughfare Gap to prevent Confederate units from crossing the Bull Run Mountains. Gibbons Division was stationed in the gap to stop all movement and when Division commander Gibbon heard that Brigadier General Owen had permitted some civilians to pass through the lines, he exploded and arrested Owen on the spot. Colonel Dewitt Baxter of the 72nd Pa was put temporary in charge of the Brigade. On June 23, Alexander Stewart Webb, a staff officer, was promoted to Brigadier General, and it was arranged to have him replace Joshua Owen as commander of the Philadelphia Brigade. On that day Private James Devine in company F collapsed in camp. Devine, who had claimed to be 44 when he joined in 1861, was actually a 52 year old Armaugh, Ireland born laborer. He had been injured in camp back in January, 1863 and now could no longer keep up with the regimental march. He was diagnosed back in Washington DC as "Old Age, varicose veins of right leg & chronic Rheumatism . . . unfit for duty" **11**

The same day, Sergeant Cornell McGlinchy of company C took sick and had to be sent back to a Washington DC hospital. McGlinchy had taken sick before down on the Peninsula in August 1862 and required a month of recuperation before fighting at Antietam. The 36 Tyrone born Sergeant stood at 5' 10" and had served in three-month service before joining the 69th in August 1861. Private William O'Rourke took sick and was sent back to Fairfax Station for care.

Meanwhile Doctor Frederick Burmeister had been placed in charge of the Ambulance Corps. He recalled that "The weather was very hot, the roads dusty from excessive dry weather, fires raging all around from the burning of trees and underbrush. No water for man or beast and the country through which we were passing desolate." **12**

Sometime during the day, Doctor Burmeister fainted and fell off his horse, injuring his head. He was taken to an ambulance and when camp was reached treated for physical exhaustion.

Doctor Frederick Burmeister—Chief Surgeon

June 24th found the 69th was spent in camp as the 71st and 106th did picket duty. The weather was hot and humid again. Then on the morning of June 25[th,] Confederate forces probed the union skirmish lines on the west side of the mountains. The night before, the 69th and the 72nd Pa had been sent out to picket duty, and they received the first fire from the rebels. Soon, the 71st and the 106th were dispatched to reinforce the line. The Philadelphia brigade was in a battle line for the next few hours, but no major attack ever came. That morning the Division was ordered to march to Edwards Ferry to cross the Potomac. General Hooker now knew that Lee's Army was heading toward Pennsylvania. Rode's Confederates were already in Chambersburg.

The Second Division was at the rear of the Second Corps march by the morning of June 25th, and the Philadelphia Brigade was selected to serve as rear guard of the division. The column moved toward the village of Haymarket and then drew up in a battle line to give the rest of the Corps and Division time to move toward the Potomac River. About a mile outside town, a Confederate horse artillery battery, belonging to Jeb Stuart opened up on the Brigade line but Union counter fire soon chased off the rebel guns. At this point Stuart fatefully turned south to go around the Army of the Potomac.

There were no injuries in the 69th from the rebel fire and soon the column was through the village of Haymarket and heading overland for village of Gum Springs. In those days there was no road to Gum Springs and the 69th had to walk through wet fields for many hours to reach the hamlet. That night, about 11:00PM, the 69th slept along side a creek beside Belmont ridge.

Meanwhile, back in Philadelphia Private Patrick Anderson from company A was preparing to rejoin his regiment. Anderson had been captured at the battle of Antietam and had spent three weeks as a prisoner in Richmond before being paroled October 6. He was sent to Camp Parole where he recovered from sickness until February 1863 and was sent home to Philadelphia to recover completely. Because of a mix-up in communications, the unmarried railroad worker remained in Philadelphia awaiting orders which never came until early June when he was told to rejoin the 69th at Falmouth camp. Another odyssey began as Anderson took the train to Baltimore only to learn on June 25th that the Second Corps was already marching north. Somehow, he would find his way to the railroad line that headed to York Pennsylvania and took the train hoping to met up with his regiment there. On the afternoon of July 1, the train he was riding would be stopped by Confederate cavalry and he would again become a prisoner of war. Anderson would escape from rebel hands in Feb 1865 and return to his regiment at Petersburg. He would be mustered out of the service on July 1 but rejoin the army in June 1866. He served with the 30th US Infantry out west in company G for three years then moved to Chicago where he would die in 1912.

The date of June 25th would be important to all of the men in the 69th and to the legacy of the regiment as well. The Union High Command issued specific instructions on that date regarding the rules and regulations with regard to reenlistment of individuals and regiments into the army at the time when their regular three years service ended. General Order Number 191 was issued by the War Department.

GENERAL ORDERS NO. 191.
WAR DEPT., ADJT. GENERAL'S OFFICE,
Washington, June 25, 1863.
FOR RECRUITING VETERAN VOLUNTEERS.

In order to increase the armies now in the field, volunteer infantry, cavalry, and artillery may be enlisted, at any time within ninety days from this date, in the respective States, under the regulations hereinafter mentioned. The volunteers so enlisted, and such of the three years' troops now in the field as may re-enlist in accordance with the provisions of this order, will constitute a force to be designated "veteran volunteers." The regulations for enlisting this force are as follows:

I.   The period of service for the enlistments and re-enlistments above mentioned shall be for three years or during the war.

II. All able-bodied men between the ages of eighteen and forty-five years, who have heretofore been enlisted, and have served for not less than nine months, and can pass the examination required by the Mustering Regulations of the United States, may be enlisted under this order as *veteran volunteers*, in accordance with the provisions hereinafter set forth.

III. Every volunteer enlisted and mustered into service as a veteran under this order shall be entitled to receive from the United States one months pay in advance, and a bounty and premium of $402, to be paid as follows:

1.   Upon being mustered into service he shall be paid one month's pay in advance $13 First installment of bounty $25 premium 2 Total payment on muster $40

2. At the first regular pay-day, or two months after muster-in, an additional installment of bounty will be paid $50

3. At the first regular pay-day after six months' service he shall be paid an additional installment of bounty 50

4. At the first regular pay-day after the end of the first year's service additional installment of bounty will be paid $50

5. At the first regular pay-day after eighteen months" service an additional installment of bounty will be paid $50

6. At the first regular pay-day after two years' service an additional installment of bounty will be paid $50

7. At the first regular pay-day after two years and a half years' an additional installment of bounty will be paid $50

8. At the expiration of three years' service the remainder of the bounty will be paid $75

IV. If the Government shall not require these troops for the full period of three years, and they shall be mustered honorably out of service before the expiration of their term of enlistment, they shall receive, upon being mustered out, the whole amount of bounty remaining unpaid, the same as if the full term had been served. The legal heirs of volunteers who die in the service shall be entitled to receive the whole bounty remaining unpaid at the time of the soldier's death.

V. Veteran volunteers enlisted under this order will be permitted, at their option, to enter old regiments now in the field; but their service will continue for the full term of their own enlistment, notwithstanding the expiration of the term for which the regiment was originally enlisted. New organizations will be officered only by persons who have been in service and have shown themselves properly qualified for command. As a badge of honorable distinction, "service chevrons" will be furnished by the War Department, to be worn by the veteran volunteers.

VI. Officers of regiments whose terms have expired will be authorized, on proper application, and approval of their respective Governors, to raise companies and regiments within the period of sixty days; and if the company or regiment authorized to be raised shall be filled up and mustered into service within the said period of sixty days, the officers may be decommissioned of the date of their original commissions, and for the time engaged in recruiting they will be entitled to receive the pay belonging to their rank.

VII. Volunteers or militia now in service, whose term of service will expire within ninety days, and who shall then have been in service at least nine months, shall be entitled to the aforesaid bounty and premium of $402, provided they re-enlist, before the expiration of their present term, for three years or the war; and said bounty and premium shall be paid in the manner herein provided for other troops re-entering the service. The new term will commence from date of re-enlistment.

VIII. After the expiration of ninety days from this date volunteers serving in three-years' organizations, who may re-enlist for three years or the war, shall be entitled to the aforesaid bounty and premium of $402, to be paid in the manner herein provided for other troops re-entering the service. The new term will commence from date of re-enlistment.

IX. Officers in service, whose regiments or companies may re-enlist, in accordance with the provisions of this order, before the expiration of their present term, shall have their commissions continued, so as to preserve their date of rank as fixed by their original muster into United States service.

X. As soon after the expiration of their original term of enlistment as the exigencies of the service will permit, a furlough of thirty days will be granted to men who may re-enlist in accordance with the provisions of this order.

XI. Volunteers enlisted under this order will be credited as three-years' men in the quotas of their respective States. Instructions for the appointment of recruiting officers and for enlisting veteran volunteers will be immediately issued to the Governors of States.

By order of the Secretary of War:
E. D. TOWNSEND,
Assistant Adjutant-General.
124 OR 415-416 **13**

Although most of the men in the 69th would not have three year terms ending until the following July 1864, this General Order would loom in the minds of most over the next year.

The next morning, the26th of June at 5:30AM, the Brigade was on the road through Cub Run again heading toward Edward's Ferry on the Potomac some 6 hours away. The distance was about 14 miles and two pontoon bridges awaited their crossing. The wagon train had taken longer to reach the pontoon bridges having to take some dirt roads from Haymarket (Gum Springs Road and Belmont Ridge Road). Sometime that day, Private John Gallagher, in company K deserted and never crossed the river with his regiment. Gallagher,21 and 6 foot tall, who had missed the Fredericksburg battle because of a cut foot, had been a burnisher before the war. By the time the wagons crossed the pontoons it was almost dark, and the 69th crossed over and made camp along the Potomac River. When they finished crossing, the ten boys and men of the 69th fife & drum corps helped them march in time to camp. The "Irish Volunteers" were close to Poolesville Maryland where they had spent the winter of 1861-1862. The 69th entered Poolesville by noon and then marched on to Barnesville, Maryland where they spent the night of June 27th-June 28th. The next morning was Sunday, and the men were on the march by 9:00AM towards Urbana. Private Samuel Hammond deserted company K and would be left behind near Frederick. Hammond had deserted twice before. The first time, just before the battle at Glendale when he ended up being captured by Confederate cavalry. The second time on the road from Chain Bridge to Centreville back in September 1862, he was Court Martialed and then returned to the regiment. His captain, William Davis, wrote on his military file "Has never yet been in an engagement, has always been noted for an habitual straggler." **14**

Back in Philadelphia, with rebels in York and Carlisle counties, panic spread throughout the city with rumors that soon Confederate troops would be marching down Broad Street. The fear of actual rebel invasion marked the beginning of decline of the Democratic "Peace Party". Power in the local Democratic Party had been shifting slowly toward the "pro-war" faction headed by Irish Catholic Lewis Cassidy over the past several years. The Keystone Club, which housed the pro-war Democrats had been lead by William McMullen. It soon became the centre of Democratic power in city politics, eclipsing the Central Democratic Club, home of the Peace Democrats.

As the 69th "Irish Volunteers" marched along toward Frederick, the word spread among the lads that General George Meade had replaced General Joseph Hooker. The Philadelphia Brigade would now have a fellow Pennsylvanian as their Army Commander with Hancock from Norristown as their Corps commander. Time after time, both North and South, commanders found that this "same state" policy had a markedly positive effect on a brigades morale and efficiency. Unfortunately what was most on the mind of the 69th was this new Brigade commander Alexander Stewart Webb from New York, a 28-year-old West Point graduate who had replaced their beloved Joshua Owens. Owens was still with the Brigade as it marched north, but under house arrest. Brigadier General Webb was determined to tighten up on discipline and take firm control of the Philadelphia Brigade, especially the Irishmen in the 69th. Webb arrived in camp as it was being prepared along the Monocacy River east of Frederick Maryland, near the railroad junction and the Frederick turnpike. The 69th was stationed to the north on the right flank of the Corps along the Monocacy. During the day, Commissary Sergeant Hugh Logan had been hurt while trying the turn a wagon. His left leg got caught between two wagons and the result was abrasions and torn muscles. He was send to the Frederick hospital and then to West Philadelphia hospital for a month's care.

While in the Frederick area, a total of eight men from company F reported to the brigade hospital and would be included among the sick on the June 30th muster report. However, research shows that at least all but one of these men were back with the regiment when it entered Gettysburg July 2nd. The sole exception may be Private Henry Gilpin who appears on the Frederick sick list June 30th and also appears to have been in the same Frederick Hospital on July 8th. Gilpin's name does appear on the 69th's plaque on the Pennsylvania Monument at Gettysburg and therefore I credit him as having been present at the battle. He may well have caught up with the regiment, fought in the battle and then took sick and ended back in the same Frederick, Maryland hospital.

When the men of the 69th first laid their eyes on their new Brigade commander, they held their tongues. Here was a man without any combat experience who dressed like a dandy. A man who openly talked and wrote about his disrespect for the Irish soldier. A man who had already decided to be a harsh disciplinarian with his new Brigade.

Webb would soon get his chance to bring "order" to the Brigade and to show the Irish of the 69th who was boss. On the morning of the 29th, the 2nd

Corps had gotten an early start on the road to Uniontown Maryland but the Philadelphia Brigade had not yet started. General Webb called his staff together and informed the Regimental leaders that he was going to catch-up with the rest of the Corps by marching to the east in a wide arc that would place the Brigade back in line with the rest of the Division. He decided that the Philadelphia brigade would march five miles to the east overland after crossing the Monocacy River, avoiding the main road, and then ford the Monocacy again and race to the village of Liberty to regain its place in line. As it turned out, Webb's first experience at leadership was a failure; by the time the brigade got across the river ford and reached the road, the rest of the Corps was already approaching Liberty. Webb's arrogant behavior during this little episode put a bad taste in the mouth of the men of the 69th. When the troops reached the knee deep river ford that Webb planned for them to cross, they began top take off their brogans and stockings When Webb saw this he jumped from his horse in the middle of the river and ordered the men to cross the river without removing their brogans. A number of veterans expressed their opinions aloud at his disregard for the blistering effects of marching in wet brogans and several pointed out that Webb's boots extended above the water level. The Second Corps had stopped for a rest in Liberty and, by nightfall, the Corps had passed through Johnsville, Mount Pleasant and Union Bridge. The Philadelphia Brigade was back in line as they would have been without Webb's shortcut. One can only imagine the conversations around the campfire that night outside Unionville, Maryland about Webb's boots, wet brogans and the "arrogant dandy" they now had as commander. The 69th had marched 31 miles in one day. It had been a day of what Charles Banes would call "tramping through the stifling dust under a burning sun, in heavy marching order" 15 During that day Private Michael Kavanaugh, born in Wexford, Ireland dropped out of the march and was taken by wagon to a hospital in Frederick, Maryland with heat prostration. The 32 year old former waterman from company B, would be sent to Philadelphia and return to the regiment in March 1864. That evening Assistant Surgeon Elwood Corson came down with the symptoms of Typhoid fever and was rushed to the Frederick Hospital and then sent to Philadelphia. He would resign his commission in September. The medical staff was dwindling.

In the town of Frederick the Provost Guard apparently failed to close down the town taverns and the next day, after marching through the city, a number of drunken stragglers filled the road trying to catch up with their regiments. All along the roads, through each little village, citizens appeared waving American Flags and handing out food and greetings. Some saw the opportunity for making a profit from the marching army. General Wainwright noted "the people along the road sell everything, and at a high price . . . fifty cents for a large loaf of bread, worth say twenty, fifteen to twenty cents for a canteen, three pints, of skimmed milk; how much for pies I do not know . . ." **16**

The citizens of Pennsylvania and Maryland were alarmed. By late June 1863 it was clear that the Army of Northern Virginia had been able to march north unimpeded and invade. Harrisburg and Baltimore, even Philadelphia, seemed threatened. The Army of the Potomac, and with it the 69th Pa, had rushed north to close on the rebel army. During this time the Second Corps and the Second Division broke records for marching speed (36 miles on one day). Some days saw the troops hike more than 25 miles in full gear with men fainting and dying along the way. On they marched through Union Bridge and into Uniontown.

On the morning of the 30th of June, the lads of "Paddy Owen's regulars" found themselves sleeping in a field owned by the Babylon family one mile beyond Uniontown. The exact position of the invading Confederate army not being known, orders were given to halt the Second Corps at Uniontown and wait until the artillery and wagon trains were brought up before proceeding. The First Corps under Reynolds and the Eleventh Corps under Howard would move ahead to a small town called Gettysburg, just across the Pennsylvania border.

Meanwhile, it was payday. The muster was taken and the numbers of men who had dropped out were counted. The morning brought two months back pay to the troops and a day's rest for weary legs, backs and feet. Time to dry brogans and stockings, repair clothing and tend to the leathers. With Commissary Sergeant Logan absent, Quartermaster Sergeant Draper Smith worked with Acting Regimental Commissary Sergeant Isaac Van Zant, Privates Hugh McAfee, Sylvester Sossaman and John Prenderville to prepare three day rations to be placed in haversacks. Over at the Brigade commissary, the slaughtering of beef and pigs and baking of bread was aided by detached men of the 69th: John Flood, John McLane and William Sullivan. The men of the 69th slept and ate and wondered what the next days would bring them. In Company G, Captain Hugh Boyle continued sick and would have to ride in a wagon for the rest of the trip north. He was still suffering from an abscess in his left groin, which had been caused by his wounds at Antietam. All of the marching since the regiment left Falmouth had taken a toll on the Captain and he would be unable to fight with his company at the upcoming battle. Command of the company would fall to First Lieutenant Bernard Sherry.

The June 30th muster shows Captain Hugh Boyle of company G as "sick" and not present for action. His condition would not improve over the next several days.

On the 30th, a number of changes were made to the detached status of the regiment. Private Henry Schwartz was detached from company G to the Hospital Staff. William Fleming, from the same company, was detached as hostler for Dr Frederick Burmeister and would remain with him during the battle.

The muster records of the 69th dated "near Uniontown, Md. June 30, 1863" told the story of the number left behind since May 30th's last muster call. The active strength of the 69th Pa on May 30th had been 389 men. 14 had been left behind in hospitals sick when the regiment headed north from Falmouth, Va. on June 14th. Along the way north another 21 men had dropped out sick, injured or deserted. This left 354 reporting for duty on June 30th. Of course "Paddy Owen" was still with the regiment relieved from command and under strict orders to not go into any battle action with the 69th.

Two General Orders were issued by General Meade on June 30th. The first was instructions for all regiments to issue three days rations and 60 rounds of ammunition to all troops.

The two butchers John McLane and John Prenderville went to work slaughtering cattle to prepare meat rations,. The regimental cooks, John Flood, William Sullivan, Joseph Crook and Sylvester Prenderville began baking and cooking food for the haversacks.

With Hugh Logan missing Quarter Master Sergeant Draper Smith and Captain Thomas Kelly took care of the ammunition distribution.

The second General order was to instruct the regimental commanders to "address their troops, explaining to them briefly the immense issues involved in the struggle". At the end of the Order came this instruction . . . .

"Corps and other commanders are authorized to order the instant death of any soldier who fails in his duty at this hour."

The next incident that would be recalled by those who grew to resent Brigadier General Webb occurred late in the afternoon of the day of rest at the Babylon farm. Webb assembled the officers of the four regiments of the Philadelphia Brigade and began the meeting by insulting the group for being out of officer dress and told them to wear their officer's insignia as they prepared for the coming battle. Webb, the man who had never seen combat, seemed unaware that, long ago, officers had learned advertising one's rank to enemy sharpshooters was an unhealthy practice. Webb made it clear that all of his officers went to Gettysburg in full dress uniform.

On Wednesday morning, July 1, the brigade prepared to march into Pennsylvania. Before starting, General Webb called all of his officers to a staff meeting where he declared that all stragglers on the march would be shot. In the 69th, this only strengthened the negative feelings about the man who had replaced "Paddy Owen". That morning Assistant Surgeon Elwood Corson's father back in Philadelphia received a message informing him of the sickness of his son and took action to bring him home and dispatched a man with the attached note . . . .

Philadelphia, July 1, 1863

R Simpson U.S.A.
Medical Director Baltimore

Dear Sir;
    I just received a dispatch from the Surgeon in charge that Dr E.M. Corson Asst. Surgeon of the 69th Penna. Vol. Is lying ill at the Genl Hospital Frederick, Md—I will send the bearer to bring him home if possible. Can you please assist this effort?

Dr. M Corson **17**

By 7:00 AM, the regiments were on the march to Taneytown, Maryland where they stopped for a rest. Soon the sounds of artillery came from the north towards Gettysburg and the Second Corps was ordered up, reaching Pennsylvania in late afternoon. Sometime during this march Private Cornelius O'Reilly straggled behind the column. He would not be seen again until after the Battle of Gettysburg was over. Born in Cork, O'Reilly had managed to miss every engagement since joining in August 1861. He would disappear again on the march south after Gettysburg.

Off in the distance, a few miles from where the 69th was marching another story was unfolding . . . Private Patrick Anderson, company A, was again a prisoner of war, now herded along the Lancaster—Gettysburg road with other union prisoners to an unknown fate.

The men of the 69th regiment continued through the darkness and stopped near the Jacob Weikert Farm on Taneytown Road along side a stream that crossed the road. The locals called the slope they slept on that night Weed's Hill. Close by was a large rocky mound called "Round Top". **18**

For many years after the war, a story was circulated by some of the men of the 69th that while sitting around the campfire down by the Taneytown Road on the evening of July 1, Captain Michael Duffy of Company I told his men that he had a feeling that he was going to be killed in this next fight. While such feelings are often thought and sometimes discussed by soldiers who know they are going into battle, his comrades in I company could not ever recall their captain ever speaking of such feelings before. Duffy had been in thick of it at Glendale and at Antietam. He had climbed Marye's Heights at Fredericksburg and had survived all the shot and shell at each of these battles. His prediction seems to have made a mark in the minds of several of his men that night. Years later a story was told by some of the men of the 69th about a scene that occurred around the campfire that night. It seems that Captain Thompson of company F suddenly stood up and said to his men "Well, boys I shouldn't wonder if I leave you tomorrow, and when I do it will be quick" **19**

Captain Michael Duffy—Company I

Before dawn, July 2, the men of the 69th were awakened and placed in line. The company and regimental wagons had been unloaded the night before and along with the teamsters and detached soldiers, sent south for protection. The morning muster would show 31 officers and 281 men reporting for battle duty. Sometime during the night Private Benjamin Story, from Company K, had left camp and deserted. Story was a 20-year-old Philadelphia born soldier who had been a bookbinder by trade before the war. He had been with the regiment since the beginning of the war and had served in all the battles. The regiment would never see him again.

For several hours, the 2nd Division stood at the ready waiting for General Gibbons return from his conference with Hancock. During this time Webb again spoke to the brigade, this time directly to the men themselves. During the pause, on May 30 Colonel O'Kane had asked for a report from each company on the numbers of men who had been lost from the previous muster. Each First Sergeant prepared the written report. Company A showed four men missing Private Patrick Hewitt a deserter and Sergeant James White and Privates Dan Crowley and John Curtin sick in hospitals. Company B also had four missing men Two deserters Private Charles Bettinger and Thomas Reardon as well as two men who had been detached and detailed. Private Charles Dorrington to the provost and Private Hugh McCall to the Corps Headquarters. Company C also had four names to report, all sick and left behind. Sergeant William Rourke and Privates Cornell McGlinchy, James Campbell and James Reynolds. Company D had four dropouts as well, Privates James McPeak, William Paugh, Michael Roach and Dennis Murray all sick and left behind along the march. Company E had two deserters, Privates John Meade and Martin Riley plus on musician, William Collins who was sick in DC. In Company F there were also four names. Private James Hamilton had deserted. Privates William Seary and Andrew Hugh were in Philadelphia hospitals and Private James Devin had dropped out sick along the march. Company G had the greatest number to report—9 men. Of these four were detailed and detached to the Ambulance train, Privates George Keen, Steve Boyle, Michael McCrea and Thomas Scott. The others were accounted for as sick. These included Corporal Thomas Jordan and Privates John Coakley, Alexander Collins, Patrick Garvin and Francis McLaughlin. Company H had the least number absent, only two. Private James Murphy had been detailed as a teamster and Private James McHenry

Had been discharged from the service. Company I had one man detailed with the teamsters; one sick in the hospital, Private Alfred Hill and four deserters, Privates John Frazier, George Melvin, John Frank, and James

Branigan—for a total of six. And finally in Company K six names were turned in. Private John Robinson was under arrest back in Washington DC. Private David Bruce was sick in a DC Hospital and five men had deserted along the march. Privates Charles Donnelly, Patrick Fox, Samuel Harmon, John Gallagher and Peter Moore. The total number of names turned in were 47, plus two men from the regimental staff, Assistant Surgeon Corson and Commissary Sergeant Hugh Logan. Colonel O'Kane must have been apprehensive as he prepared to turn in this report to Brigadier General Webb. Webb would, of course, make these 49 names the basis for new negative feelings about "His Irish". Of course the entire path of the Army of the Potomac northward was littered with sick and deserting soldiers and there is no reason believe that the 69th's loss of approximately 14 % was over the average.

In the 69th, Company H had been detailed to guard the wagons and camp when the regiment moved forward. At some point that morning General Meade himself rode up and addressed the men of the Brigade "The enemy is now on our soil. The whole country looks anxiously to this army to deliver it from the presence of the foe. Our failure to do so will leave us no such welcome as the smiling of the millions of hearts with pride and joy at our success would give to every soldier of the army." Finally at about 7:00AM, the Division had its orders and marched on an old country farm lane up to Cemetery Ridge and across the ridge to its battle position in the center of the Union "fish hook" position. **20** Left behind, of course, along the Taneytown Road was Joshua "Paddy" Owen. Later the men of the 69th would hear that he had been spotted near the Pitzer Schoolhouse reportedly being obviously very drunk.

CHAPTER THREE

JULY 2 AT GETTYSBURG

General Hancock was waiting when the Second Corps moved into position on Cemetery Ridge. He instructed Brigadier General Gibbon to place the Second Division to the south (left) of the Third Division under Brigadier General Alexander Hayes. The brigade order from right to left would be Webb, then Hall, then Harrow. Hayes' men from New York, New Jersey and Connecticut would have protection behind a large stone wall that ran from north to south near the crest of the hill. Behind them would be the artillery of Arnold and Woodruff. The men of the 69th noticed, at once, that they would be defending a smaller wall that was 90 yards out front of the crest, a wall joined to the crest wall to their right by a connecting wall topped by a rail. This would place their brigade at the very front of the defensive position, the very first location to be hit in any assault on this section of the hill, called by locals "Granite Ridge". Webb went to work positioning his four regiments. The 69th would be placed at the small front wall with a regimental front of about 250 feet. Up at the crest, in reserve, would be the 71st and 72nd and 106th in that order from north to south. Whereas Hays had his front regiments and his reserves evenly divided. Webb had chosen to have only one of his four regiment, the 69th "Irish" at the battlefront. As Webb gave his commands to his Colonels, the lads of the 69th noticed that Company G was at the left flank position of the line usually occupied by Company K because Company H had rushed to catch up with the regiment after being put on wagon guard detail that morning. The result was that the normal marching regimental formation was thrown off, hence the formation of the battle line was thrown off as well. As John McKeever of company E testified in the 72nd Pa vs Gettysburg Monument

Commission, "I think that company H was on the left of our regiment on that day. I believe that company H was next to company K (in double company marching line) because they had been detailed on the march and they fell in there." 1

Next to Webb's Brigade was Hall's Brigade with the 59th New York on the left flank of the 69th. The 59th New York had been badly mauled at Chancellorsville and had been reduced and consolidated to a four company regiment. Many of its officers had resigned or had been court-martialed amid a scandal involving stolen funds in the past two months. The men in the 69th must have hoped that the 59th was ready as a unit for the coming fight.

Webb's selection of the 69th to be the sole regiment at his brigade front presented the "Irish Volunteers" with a topography problem. The wall section they would be defending was in a sorry condition, not having been kept in repair in recent times. The wood fence rail on top of the wall was in complete disrepair. It was clear that local farmers had used the area for some time as a dumping ground. To make matters more challenging, a cluster or copse of small trees was growing up toward the crest from the wall, and small bushes and trees grew all the way down to the wall itself. In order to make room for the ten companies that would occupy the 250-foot wall front, many of these small trees would have to be chopped down and shrubs up rooted. This wood would be used to rebuild a fence rail on top of the two-foot high wall. The use of the area as a dumping ground was clear from the broken wagon wheels, discarded lumber, large stones and various debris that was scattered around the position of the 69th. As the men took up positions, they saw that they had work to do on their advanced location. The regimental line ran downhill from right to left, and so the 69th Pa found itself below the crest of the ridge and below the right of their own line. In many ways, they had been placed in a hole behind a wall. Behind the left end of the line was a small outcropping of rocks that would be at the back of companies G and K. This would be troublesome because the rocks would hinder any backward motion and would pose a potential danger for slipping and falling. Finally the left flank of the regiment could not see any approaching enemy units until these units were almost on top of them.

The companies of the 69th were arranged from right to left in the following order I, (the traditional right flank company), A,F,D,H,C (The color company), E,B,K (the traditional left flank company and finally Company G. When the detached men and musicians were sent to the rear, a total of 312 men were prepared to fight at the wall on July 2. "After establishing the line of battle, a detail of two men was taken from each company, and added to details from the other three regiments of the brigade, and were placed on picket a little beyond Emmittsburg Pike" to the west. **2**

As the 69th prepared its position, the artillery batteries that would give them support were wheeled into position. To their right and rear would be the 6 guns of Cushing's Battery (Battery A 4th US Artillery) and to their left on the south side of the copse of trees would be the 6 guns of Brown's battery (1st Rhode Island light Battery B). The high ground to the north or right of the 69th (which would dominate their line if ever captured), was an unoccupied space of about 135 feet kept clear for the use of Cushing's Guns. In front of The 59th New York and Brown's battery and in front of the wall was an outcropping of rock that was overgrown with small trees and bushes. This had to be cleared and was cleared by the 59thNew York and the 7th Michigan and the artillerymen of Brown's battery. This "slash" could serve as potential cover for any attacker.

Private Anthony McDermott—Company I

A staff meeting was held with Colonel O'Kane, Lieutenant Colonel Tschudy, Major Duffy, Adjutant Whildey and the company commanders to review the defensive plans. Private Anthony McDermott in company I had been detailed as clerk to the Adjutant for some time and was told to stay in the rear during the coming fight. "At the time of this battle, I was a private of Co. I, which was always the first company of the Regt. But was detailed as clerk to the Adjutant. By the advice of Major Palmer who was on the Division staff as Inspector, the Adjutant took from me my rifle and accoutrements so that I could not go into battle. His object was that if the Adjt. And his clerk were both disabled it would be a difficult matter to transact the business of the Regt. Properly for some time afterward. I always disregarded these instructions and at Gettysburg, I filled my pockets with cartridges, and before noon of the 2nd I got a rifle from a wounded picket and endeavored to discharge my duty as a soldier and as an American." 3

As the men went to work clearing small trees and moving discarded farm items and building a fence rail, they heard and saw skirmish action out beyond the Emmittsburg Road to their front. Companies A & B of the 106th had been sent out to scout the rebel positions and they were exchanging rifle fire in the distance. The remainder of the morning and into the afternoon was spent on these tasks and finally the men had a chance to rest, write and read letters, and eat what food they had left in their haversacks. It was not until abut 4:00Pm that they began to see a major battle unfold off to their left down by a Peach Orchard and some houses along the Emmittsburg Road. As spectators, the men of the 69th had seen Sickle's Corps march to the west that morning and now saw Confederate Divisions thrown against the Third Corps of their army. They looked behind their lines as Caldwell's First Division of the Second Corps was rushed as reinforcements off behind them and then to their left. It was clear that Sickles Third Corps was crumbling under the weight of the rebel attack. Only the arrival of Caldwell's Division had stopped the rout.

By 4:00PM it was clear that the Federal troops to their left and front were retreating and General Gibbon decided to move forward two regiment s and one Artillery battery. He ordered the 82nd New York and the 15th Massachusetts from Hall's Brigade forward to the Codori Farm and Orchard, which was in front of Harrow's Brigade line and all the way forward about 800 feet at the Emmittsburg Road. To provide them with cover he had Brigadier General Harrow move Brown's Battery, with its 6 guns, forward behind the two regiments. In order to travel forward some 800 feet the battery had to be taken single file through a narrow space in the wall in front of the 59th New York. Several guns were placed on top of a knoll that rose out in the open field about halfway down to the Emmittsburg Road. The other 4 were placed in the field to their left. While these two regiments provided an advanced post in front of the Second Corps, they were out in the open with both flanks exposed. The 15th Mass was placed along the Emmittsburg Road to the right of the 82nd NY. The commander of the 15th was Colonel George H. Ward and the commander of the 82nd NY was Lieutenant Colonel James Huston

During the early afternoon the Confederate force facing these two regiments, under the command of Brigadier General Ambrose Wright, had moved forward skirmishers in enough strength to drive back the union skirmish line which had been posted several hundred feet to the West of the Emmittsburg Road. At this time Webb made a decision. "A few hundred yards in front of our line of battle and towards the left, a farm house and buildings were located (the Codori farm). To prevent these affording cover to the enemy, they were occupied by the brigade pioneers under Sergeant Dietrieck of the 106th, with orders to destroy them upon a signal from General Webb." 4

As Lee's offensive, conducted by Longstreet's Corps, rolled north along the Emmittsburg Road, Confederate s opposite the A.P. Hill's II Corps began their advance. Around 6:30 PM Wright rebel brigade moved forward to attack the 82nd New York and the 15 Massachusetts in their exposed position. Wrights four regiments moved across the fields and over the fences west of the Emmitsburg Road and made contact with the two Union regiments. The 2nd Georgia Battalion was in front as skirmishers with the 48th Georgia on its left, the 3rd Georgia in the center and the 22nd Georgia on the right. In the fighting, the 69th would be to the left (north) of the confederate attack. The tall grass hid the Confederate infantry advance and the Union skirmish line was no longer there to warn of the advance. The entire rebel brigade sprang upon the outnumbered men from Massachusetts and New York in an instant. With the rebel yell in the air, and a full volley from 1000 rifles, the union lines fired one volley then a second, and then the 82nd NY melted in rout. Quickly the 15th Mass was flanked on it's left and also retreated in panic. Both commanders of the regiments were mortally wounded in the fighting.

With the two Union regiments overwhelmed and in flight, Brown's guns became the next target. Wright's advance threatened to capture all six guns, but Brown was able to bring out some of his guns. One cannon was left behind on top of the knoll and another in the field, while the four others rushed for the small gap in the stone wall. The first got through, but then two crews tried to pass though at the same time and both got stuck. The final gun had to be abandoned in front of the wall. The men of the 69th lay behind their wall and watched the debacle unfold. Now, the 48th Georgia regiment was charging straight toward the 69[ths] portion of the wall. As Wright's men moved forward Confederate supporting artillery was moved toward the Emmittsburg Road and began firing shells into the Union lines. Several of these shells exploded within or above the heads of the men of the 69th Pa. At least two exploding shells seem to have found their mark within the ranks of the 69th during the cannon support fire. When we examine the casualties of the regiment on July 2, we find an abnormally high number of shell fragment deaths and wounds among the officers and noncomms who would have been more exposed behind the battle line. While the enlisted men clung to the wall for protection at least two shells exploded above or amid the rear of the company ranks. One shell seems to have exploded near the middle of the regiment line near company H hitting the head of, and killing instantly, Second Lieutenant Charles Kelly. Kelly was the 22-year-old brother of Captain Thomas Kelly, who was in Philadelphia during the Gettysburg battle. The younger brother had served a variety of posts in the regiment including butcher and Assistant Quartermaster. His brother had written letters to help Charles get a commission, which he did receive in May 1863. Charles would be send home and buried July 9th at Cathedral cemetery in West Philadelphia in a grave he would eventually share with Thomas, who would die at Spotsylvania less than a year later. To Kelly's left, Private Michael Kelly (no relation), in company D, was struck in the right shoulder with a shell fragment that put him out of action. Kelly was a 37-year-old Derry Ireland native. He was single and a laborer before the war. To Kelly's immediate left in company C, Private James McNulty was hit with several shell fragments that would result in his death on July 6th at the Field Hospital. He was a 27-year-old newcomer to the regiment, a Tyrone native who joined on January 2, 1863. Standing at the rear of company E just to the left was Captain Thomas Wood who received contusions on his right side from an exploding shell. Captain Wood had been Sergeant Wood in the "Meagher Guard Militia and also Sergeant Wood in company K of the 24th Pa. He was born in Cootehill, County Cavan, Ireland and had been a carpenter before the war. Wood's 24 year old 2nd Lieutenant John Taggart, was slightly wounded by fragments as well. Taggart, as a Sergeant, had been wounded at Antietam, had deserted from the hospital was arrested and then returned to the company to become 2nd Lieutenant.

Further to the left flank, a shell seems to have exploded over companies B and K showering fragments into the rear positions. Sergeant James McShea, of Company B, was killed instantly behind the line. He stood at the left side of the company line next to company K. McShea was a 36 year old Irishman who had joined in August 1861 but spent much of 1862 in Philadelphia working on 69th regiment recruiting duties. He returned to the regiment in Jan 1863 and was promoted from Corporal to Sergeant. He was married and had four children His wife, Sarah, would remarry his best friend 1st Sgt. John Britt (Co B) in 1868. In the same Company, Privates Andrew McGuckin and James O'Neill died instantly on the left side of the Company B position. McGuckin, age 27, had joined the regiment on August 15, 1862 and had been a plumber in Phoenixville, Pa before the war. His body would be recovered by his brother shortly after the battle and returned home. O'Neill was 40 years old and had been in the 69th since the beginning. He had spent much time in 1862 sick in a Washington, DC hospital. He returned to company B in March. O'Neill left behind him a young child and a widow, Anna, who moved to Washington DC during his illness. Private Timothy Gallagher fell dead with a head wound sometime during the fighting. The records do not indicate whether this was a bullet wound or a shell fragment wound. Timothy Gallagher was born in Donegal, Ireland and, at the age of 25, joined the 69th PVI on the 28th of November 1861 at Camp Observation in Poolesville, Md.

After the fight, two men from Company K would be found with shell wounds. Private James Todd lay dead at the wall with a shell fragment puncture to his lungs, and Private William McNichols would report to the hospital with a shell fragment wound on his head. McNichols medical report reads "McNichols, William Pvt. Co K 69thP.V. aged 28 contusion of the left parietal by a fragment of shell, which lacerated the scalp for three inches or more at Gettysburg 7/2/63. Treated at Mower hospital on August 14th, an exfoliation of the outer table was removed and the patient recovered and was returned to duty on 12/16/1863." 5 McNichols, a veteran of company E of the 24th PVI, served with the 69th regiment since August 1861, was captured at Savage Station and paroled at Aiken's Landing August 5. After his Gettysburg wounding, he would suffer brain damage that caused epileptic convulsions. After the war his doctor reported that he had "fits" and acted "idiotic". Private James Todd, a Dover, Maryland farmer died instantly of wounds to his lungs. Todd was the sole support for his crippled father, his mother having died in 1852.

At some point in the fight, Lieutenant Colonel Martin Tschudy was struck in the head by either a bullet or piece of shell fragment. The object grazed the right side of his head causing a contusion. Out at the road, most of the "pioneers" from the 69th had been captured and placed inside the Codori barn under guard.

Lieutenant Colonel Martin Tschudy

Despite this violent cannonade, the "Irish Volunteers" held firm at the wall and prepared to open up on the advancing rebels. McDermott wrote about the volley of fire that sprang from the wall "We met their charge with such a destroying fire that they were forced back in confusion. They rallied again and make a second effort and again their lines are broken and thinned as we pour volley upon volley into their disorganized lines and they finally retired a dispirited mob, not even able to take Brown's abandoned guns which they twice succeeded in reaching." 6

At one point, the rebels had reached as far as the abandoned cannon just outside the gap in the wall and had fought hand to hand with the 59th New York. Suddenly, a rebel officer in clear view ordered his men to turn around Brown's abandoned gun on the knoll and load it. Captain Michael Duffy of Company A saw this and jumped on top of the wall and shouted "Knock that damned officer off that gun". Duffy was struck in the mouth with a minie ball as he finished his order. 7 Duffy was well loved by his men and had been instrumental in organizing the 69th back in 1861. He owned a tavern on Broad Street where the Irishmen of the 69th gathered. He had been Captain of Company A of the 24th in 1861.

There is no evidence that any of Brown's cannons were ever used by the confederate troops and all were recovered after the counterattack. During these two attacks 10 more men of the regiment were hit by gunfire. Especially hard hit were two of the companies on the left flank K and B. The new wing company G seems to have kept themselves well protected. Only Private Patrick Noonan was hit of the Company G men. Noonan, who had been wounded in the head at Glendale, took a bullet, which entered his chest halfway between his left nipple and his sternum and traveled downward lodging two inches below his left nipple. Noonan was probably leaning over loading his rifle when the bullet struck. The Private, who had been a letter writer for many in the company would recover and serve out his three year term.

With the exception of Captain Duffy, who had made himself an easy target by jumping on top of the stone wall, there was only one rifle fire casualty among the five right companies in the fight. A bullet hit Private Stephen Sullivan in Company D three inches below the right elbow as he aimed and fired his rifle along the wall. Captain James Harvey and Charles McAnally had recruited him into company D in Danville, Pa back in August 1861. The 29-year-old Sullivan would survive after being sent to Mower Street hospital and Chestnut Hill Hospitals in Philadelphia. The Cork, Ireland born puddler before the war, would desert from that hospital twice in the next 3 months and finally be discharged for disability. After the war he would move to a Soldiers Home in Quincy, Ill and be given a pension.

Company B was especially hard hit by rifle fire. Not only had they lost men to exploding artillery shells, they would also have five men down with bullet wounds. At some point during the two rebel attacks, a volley must have been fired at Company B at a time when many of the men were exposed. Second Lieutenant John McIlvane, who had been promoted amid controversy back in April, was hit on the right arm near the shoulder. He would be spun around and taken out of action. He would spend the next day at the field hospital and have problems through the fall with abscesses and, eventually, deafness caused by infection. Private Frank McGill, who had joined the regiment at age 33 in August 1862, was hit by a bullet three inches above his elbow on the right arm as he was aiming his rifle. The bullet would tear upward ripping his arm muscle and fracturing his humerus. In a few days, gangrene would set in but McGill would survive and be transferred to the Invalid Corps in Washington DC. For the rest of his life, the former carpenter would lose the use of the arm. McGill was married and had one child before he was wounded. Later, he and his wife, Alice, would have eight more. Private Joseph Grover, age 28 and a former shoemaker, was hit in the lower third of the left arm with damage to his elbow joint. He would recover in a Philadelphia hospital but desert from his hospital bed in December 1863. Private Nicholas Farrell from Newark New Jersey had been born in Ireland and joined the 69th at age 25. He was wounded in the left leg at Fredericksburg which left him with a limp and at Gettysburg had three pieces of buckshot enter his right knee. Most of the Confederates in the 48th Georgia were equipped with new buck and ball .69 caliber smoothbores from England that had been purchased from blockade runners by the Georgia Legislature. Dr. Burmeister would treat the painful injury that evening. Finally, Private Luke Meiley was hit in the hand during the fight. He wandered off away from the regiment after the fight on day 2 and was not seen again until after the three day battle was over. He was reported as a deserter on the muster records after that date.

Finally in company K, two men were hit. 21 year old Private William Hackett took a bullet in the right arm. The former hatter recovered at Satterlee hospital in Philadelphia. During his long recovery he married Hannah Harp of Wilmington Delaware. He later had a son, Robert and settled in Swedesboro, New Jersey. The final casualty in Company K was a tragic tale indeed. Corporal Henry Murray, age 28, was struck in the left eye by a minie ball which penetrated deep into the orbit, destroying the optic nerve. The former bookbinder would be blinded for life. As the battle ended, his good friend John Buckley would lead him back to the aid station. Buckley later wrote abut the event "I was in the one position during both charges, and only time I left it was when I led Sergt Murray to the rear, with both eyes shot out, and begging me, to put an end to that existence which he thought would be no longer endurable." 8 Murray would spend the next 12 months in military hospitals before being discharged. After the war he would find a reason to live marrying Hannah Jones and moving with her to Cleveland, Ohio, dying there in 1884.

As the rebels broke and began to run back toward the Emmittsburg Road and the woods across the fields, the men of the 69th looked behind their lines and saw the 106th Pennsylvania had been ordered to sweep to the right around their position and counterattack. This counterattack broke the back of the Wright attack and the entire area in front was soon cleared of Confederate troops. All that remained was the estimated more than 150 killed, 300 wounded and 150 captured of Wright's Brigade, their bodies and their discarded rifles and equipment lying all over the field. During the counterattack "The men of the 69th were eager to give pursuit but were prevented by Gens. Harrow, commanding the division and Webb, commanding the brigade." **9**

. . . . McDermott quotes one writer who summarized the fight this way . . ." the gallant Sixty-ninth under the command of Dennis O'Kane, receive the advancing foe—Wright's Brigade—with a defiant shout, as they shake out the folds of their green flag and pour a withering fire at short range into the faces of their adversaries, then backward propelled by another volley, the men in gray and butternut uniforms in confusion are driven down the slope and across the ground over which they had charged." **10** In his report to General Lee, Wright claimed to have broken the Union lines but that he had to retreat because of lack of support. This seems to have added to lee's view that the Union center was weak.

Now the battlefield grew quiet, the fighting at their front was over, The fighting at the Wheatfield and the Peach Orchard was over. Dark was settling in and darkness would soon follow. The killed and the wounded of the July 2 fighting were taken by Ambulance crews and by the musicians back down to the Field Hospital set up in the red Frey barn along the Taneytown Road. Surgeon Burmeister and Assistant Surgeon O'Neill were busy taking care of those who had been hit with artillery fragments and with bullets. The barn was soon filled with men in agonizing pain. Lieutenant Colonel Tschudy had his head bandaged and treated and then moved back up toward the wall. He was not going to be slowed by a graze on his head. The fighting had cost the 69th 7 killed in action. Some 12 others were seriously wounded and another 5 were wounded but capable of playing a role if needed the next day.

Out in front of the wall several hundred bodies of killed or seriously dead or dying Confederate and Federal troops lay in the evening coolness. The temperature began to drop and the men of the 69th still at the wall began to hear movement of troops on their own side of the wall. Companies A & B of the 106th were out on picket duty along the Emmittsburg Road but the other eight companies had been ordered to move to support Union batteries on Cemetery Hill to the north. The men of the 106th marched out just as darkness fell. Then the 71st was ordered to march off to East Cemetery Hill and they were gone. The men of the 69th must have looked at each other and wondered . . . . "Where is the rest of our Brigade? Are we all alone here at the front wall without any support (except the 72nd Pa) ???" But already the 69th was busy with another task. One by one and in small groups, careful of rebel sharpshooter fire, they went out on the battlefield amidst all the bodies to collect discarded rifles. Corporal James Buckley of Company K remembered it best . . . .""We received a lesson from the charge of the 2nd of July, which was almost similar to Pickets only the rebs did not advance in such large numbers and did not reach the wall, although they captured a battery about forty yards in our front and advanced within ten feet of the wall. We charged and recaptured the battery and took a great many prisoners, mostly of whom were Georgians, and the best clothes soldiers that we had ever come across on their side. After taking care of the wounded and removing them back, we gathered the guns and ammunition of the dead. This is the point I want to give you and show exactly what use we made of the spare guns. We kept the best—and reloaded, and reclined them against the wall. The ammunition we gathered was found to contain three buck shot and ball cartridges if, my memory does not fail me. The ammunition had a label showing it had been manufactured in Birmingham, England. and I will guarantee it brought more harm upon them than upon us, we abstracted the buckshot from the ammunition and reloaded the spare guns putting 12 to the load, and almost every man had from two to five guns that were loaded and were not used until Pickett got within fifty yards of the wall, the slaughter was terrible, to which fact—the ground was literally covered with the enemy's dead bore ample testimony." **11**

Many historians have noted that the 69th Pa was armed with a surplus of rifles as the rebels approached the wall on July 3rdand was therefore able to direct a heavy fire upon the attacking Confederates. These historians note that the extra rifles came as a result of the men of the 69th being able to go out onto the fields in front of their position and gather rifles discarded by Wright's Brigade in their charge on July 2nd. The traditional source of this occurrence is usually statements made in the letter from John Buckley (company K-69th Pa) to John Bachelder cited above.

In addition to the Buckley citation, we also have three separate statements from Richard Penn Smith, commander of the 71st Pa, regarding extra rifles. On November 25, 1867, in a letter to Peter Rothermal, publisher of the Pennsylvania Historical and Museum Commission collection, Smith states "having a large pile of loaded guns by our side." (Richard Penn Smith to Peter Rothermal, November 25th, 1867, Robert Broke Collection, U.S. Army Military History Institute, Carlisle, Pa) In 1887 in a letter to the Gettysburg

Compiler, June 7, 1887, Smith states "I directed officers and men to take from a pile of muskets, collected by my regiment on the previous day, as many capped or loaded guns as they could carry, and the officers and men of that portion of the regiment went into position behind a stone wall with from three to a dozen loaded guns each . . . ." (Richard Penn Smith, "The Battle", Gettysburg Compiler June 7, 1887). In a letter to Issac Wister Smith claims he had "300 extra guns which lay on the field" (Robert Penn Smith to Issac Jones Wister, July 29, 1863, Library of Wistar Institute Collection, Philadelphia, Pa)

The question must be asked: How could there have been enough discarded rifle-muskets laying around the field to the East of Emmitsburg Pike to provide some 500-700 rifles to the 69th Pa and an additional 600 or more to the 71st Pa. It seems that the stories exaggerated the number of extra rifles that were available that day. A close look at the losses of Brigadier General Ambrose R Wright's Brigade shows a total of 184 men killed, 343 men wounded and 169 men missing for a total of about 700 men. Now knowing that some of the casualties occurred out in the fields west of the Emmittsburg Pike and knowing that some of the wounded likely returned with their arms, we can not explain more than 500-600 extra rifles gathered. (Bradley M. Gottfried, "Wright's Charge on July 2, 1863", Gettysburg Magazine 17, 70-82)Even if we include some of the rifles lost by the two Union regiments overrun by Wright (The 15th Massachusetts and the 82nd New York—with about 320 in killed, wounded and captured) My estimate of the available "extra" rifles is about 500 or which both the 69th and the 71st could have gathered several hundred each. This would give the men of the left companies of the 69th from two to three extra each and the men at the rear wall with the 71st several extra each.

As it grew late, the men of the 69th began to fall asleep. Resting against the stone wall wrapping blankets around themselves in the cool night air, they slept and prepared for the next day of combat. Some of the men of the 69th were still awake to hear the sounds of the 71st Pa returning from their mission. Sometime early in the morning, the 71st Pa arrived back at the crest of the hill and stacked arms and tried to get some sleep. Some men from the 69th walked back to see what had happened and learned a tale of confusion and chaos. It seemed that the plan to bring the 71st to east Cemetery Hill had resulted in the entire regiment getting lost in the dark and traveling too far south up the slopes of Culp's hill instead. When they arrived at Culp's Hill, they were ordered into line with a group of New York troops who were under attack in the dark. Somehow, it seemed the 71st put out a skirmish line of companies I and F under the command of their Adjutant and then all hell broke lose. The men of the 69th were told a story of confusion and chaos in the dark as most of the 71st's picket line was captured and the regiment was fired upon from the front and right and rear. It seems that Colonel Smith decided right then and there that he was not going to be annihilated in the dark and so he, without orders, ordered his regiment to march back toward the east, across Baltimore Pike and across Taneytown road and find their way back to the copse of trees and the Crest of the hill. The confusion had cost the 71st their Adjutant, two Lieutenants and eleven men from companies F & I killed, wounded or captured in the dark. Soon, all the soldiers of the 72nd, 71st and the 69th were asleep. There would be 292 men in Paddy Owen's Regulars at the wall to face "Johnny Reb" in the morning. But for another man, Patrick Anderson, another totally different adventure was beginning. He was a prisoner of war with the confederate cavalry, having been taken on his way to rejoin his regiment. Again he would be removed from his comrades in company A of "Paddy Owen's Regulars". More men of the 69th would join him as prisoners of war within two days, but now Patrick Anderson was being marched off to a prison pen.

CHAPTER FOUR

JULY 3 GETTYSBURG THE MUSTER CALL

History records what the 69th did at the wall against Picket's Division on July 3rd. What we need to remember, however, was that the 69th was a unit made up of unique individuals whose diverse lives somehow brought them together here at a critical time just south of a small Pennsylvania town called Gettysburg.

Muster Call for Company I, at the far right of the 69th line, began with a somber note, as every man was keenly aware of the death of their Captain, Michael Duffy in the fighting the day before. Most had walked back down the hill to the Fry barn where he lay dead and was buried the evening before.

Duffy had been with them since the beginning, first as Sergeant, and then as Lieutenant. The original captain, Dan Gillen, captured at Antietam, had never recovered from the experience and the men rallied around Duffy. Now, he was gone. As First Sergeant William Richardson called out the names, many wondered how many men would be missing the next time muster was taken. 1st Lieutenant William McNamara had been wounded in the left thigh at Fredericksburg and the exit wound below his knee would be torn during the fighting. He now commanded the company at the age of 22. 2nd Lieutenant Edward Harmon from New York City was only 24 and had worked his way up from Private. At one time, he was Sergeant Major of the regiment. First Sergeant Richardson, age 23, taking the morning muster roll, was born in Derry kept order in the company. There were four other Sergeants in company I. Sergeant Joseph Garrett, from Chester County, had been wounded early in the Peninsular campaign and had worked his way up the ranks. Sergeant Patrick McMahon, age 28, was the oldest Sergeant He had also entered the 69th as a private. Sergeant Christian Rooney, 25, from Philadelphia and Sergeant James Tooney, who would after the war become a lawyer, finished off the list of Sergeants.

Two men in the company had been detailed as clerks for the regimental staff. Anthony McDermott and John Boyle. However, both men found rifles and rejoined their company as the action began on the 2nd of July. The tallest Corporal Henry Souder, stood at the end of the line and behind him was Private George Diechler from Lancaster, Pa. Next came John Ellison, age 27, and Anthony McDermott, who after the war would be active in the 69th Survivors' Association as secretary and speaker. McDermott's tent mate, Private Thomas Diver, was a printer who was the sole support for his mother back home in Philadelphia. Corporal William White, 22, was next in line and kept a diary during the war of his adventures. He would serve in every engagement for three years without a wound. Private Patrick McDermott, born in Ireland, was one of the older soldiers in the company at 32, and would spend much of the war with sicknesses. Next in line was William Frazier who had been sick during most of 1862 and had returned to the regiment in the spring. Edward Head, age 26, had deserted the regiment in November 1862 but was arrested and sent first to Fort Delaware and then back to the 69th in the spring. By his side Corporal James Milligan had been promoted recently for his bravery under fire at the Battle of Fredericksburg. Further down the line was Private Christian Rohlfing, one of the few Germans and Lutheran members of the 69th. Rohlfing was 23 and married with two children and, in addition was the sole support of his widowed mother. John Boyle, age 22 was the sole support for his widowed mother as well, had been a clerk before the war in Philadelphia. Beside him was Frank McClarren, age 23 a Philadelphia printer. Next came Michael Logan, taken prisoner at Antietam and who rejoined the regiment to fight at Fredericksburg. To his left, was the company's oldest soldier, Benjamin Pine, age 42, had fought with the company since August of 1861 only to be later killed by "friendly artillery fire" in June of 1864 at Petersburg. The next man in line, William Elben had suffered hearing loss at Malvern Hill and became the target of cruel jokes by some of his comrades. He had been captured at Antietam and had grown increasingly deaf as the war progressed. Beside Elben stood Private Bernard Collins who served as servant to Lieutenant McNamara but in battle carried a rifle in the line like all the rest of the men. Next was Private Thomas Cloney who had already been taken prisoner twice during the war, first at Antietam and then on the picket line at Banks Ford during the Chancellorsville campaign. One of the newest members of the company was Thomas Flynn who had arrived in April 1863. Born in Ireland, he worked as a printer until joining the 69th. Corporal Thomas Davis, a transplanted Virginian, who came North to fight for the union, was at the end of the line along with Privates Francis Kelly, the second oldest at age 36, and Joseph Lehman, from Camden New Jersey, one of the few Jewish soldiers in the 69th Pa. A small gap marked the beginning of the next company. Twenty nine men would hold the line for company I but in the rear three more men were on detached service. Drummer James Quirk, age 20, would be with the musicians in the rear and two men John Prenderville the regiment butcher and Sylvester Sossaman regimental cook would remain with the wagon train.

Company A had their Captain, John McHugh, in command at Gettysburg but no Lieutenants and, because of this there is a strong chance that brevet Sergeant Major Thomas Norman, age 43, filled this function during much of the fighting at the wall. Company A was his old company, and he had already been promoted but not commissioned as its 2nd Lieutenant The absence of Lieutenants from the Company was due to the vertical movement of former Captain James Duffy to the position of Major and the promotion of 2nd Lieut. John M McHugh to his place as Captain. James Cole would have been next in line, and was a former Sergeant Major of the regiment. He had been 2nd Lieut. for a short while in May but had been Court Martialed and dismissed for drunkenness and conduct unbecoming an Officer. The 1st. Lieut. John McHugh, (different man, same name, no relation) had been appointed Captain of Company B. The roll on July 3 was taken by Sergeant Steven Dooley. Captain John McHugh, age 31, was born in Tyrone Ireland and had worked himself up from Corporal to 2nd Lieutenant to 1st Lieutenant to Captain. He had lost his brother at Antietam. Sergeant Dooley was a 30-year-old from Queens, Ireland and had served in the 24th Pa. In fact, all four of the company A Sergeants had served together in the 24th Pa. First Sergeant Ralph Rickaby was also from Queens, Ireland and had known Sergeant Dooley most of his life. Rickaby had gotten married back in September 1861 just before the regiment took the trains south to Washington. Sergeant Edward Bushel from Tipperary stood at 5' 10" and was married and a shoemaker before the war. Sergeant Dennis McGowen of Tyrone was a barkeeper before the war.

Private Dennis McGowen—Company A (postwar)

At the far right of the company line was the tallest Corporal, at 5'10", Patrick Moran a shoemaker born in County Roscommon. Beside him was the tallest man in the entire regiment, six foot four inch 27 year old Private John Harvey. Harvey was not only the tallest man in the 69th but he was the only man to serve side by side with his father. His father John Harvey Senior age 46 was a lawyer by trade and had joined the regiment with his son in August 1861, fighting in every battle by his side. The traditional battle line of the Civil War had men lined up from right to left in terms of their height. This would facilitate the ability to have the rear line fire over the heads of the front line soldiers. In front of Harvey was Thomas Standing a carpenter from Frankford, Philadelphia. Frederick Bevensted was born in Germany and spoke with a thick German accent. At age 43 he was one of the older members of the company and had been sick prior to the march north. Bartholomew Conway was born in Lancaster, England and had been wounded in the hand at Fredericksburg. To the left side of Conway were Privates Charles Allen and Francis Belflow. Belflow was a Canadian citizen who came to the United States from Montreal at the start of the war to join the 69th. Next came a man from Waterford, Ireland, John Dunn who was 41 and had been sick several times during the war. Hugh McAleer, next in line, was a weaver by trade and would have a career in the US Marines after the Civil War. The next man on the battle line was Corporal William Walton who would lead the center of the company position. Beside him would be one of the oldest members of the company, 39, Robert Crooks, a British immigrant to Philadelphia who had been wounded in the thigh during the Fredericksburg fighting. The O'Brien brothers, Patrick and William, stood side by side in position. In their early thirties, born in Limerick, Ireland, they would die together at Gettysburg. Next in line was Private Moses Granlee, 33, born in County Fermanagh, unmarried and the sole support of his widowed mother in Philadelphia. Robert Morrison,23, by Moses' side, native of Derry who had a wife and a son, William back home in Philadelphia. Robert had been thrown in the stockade in June for a run in with the Captain in which he threatened the life of McHugh. John Eckard was one of the men recruited in Danville, Pa. Beside him, George Haws of Philadelphia was a plumber before the war and served as the personal servant of Major James Duffy. The shortest man in company A, Francis Cassidy, at 5' 4", stood at the far left of the line. He was the personal servant for Captain McHugh. The two corporals at the end of the line were William Donavan from Cork and Farrell McGovern from Cavan both veterans of every battle. The company drummer, John Dever, 18, remained with the musicians and Corporal John Flood was detailed at the brigade bakery with the wagon train. The men of Company A also noted the absence of several others from the battle line. Their old Captain, James Duffy, was now Major and would be positioned on the opposite end of the regimental line when combat began. They also remembered James Dunn, who as 2nd Lieutenant, was killed at Antietam. 27 men stood at the wall with Company A.

The next company in line was company F under the command of Captain George Thompson. Thompson was a respected officer among all of the 69th companies and was especially close to Irish Nationalists in the regiment. He had been badly wounded in the foot at Glendale. Thompson had been widely supported by most of the regimental officers for the position of Major of the regiment but was passed over by the selection of James Duffy, then Captain of Company A. Thompson was a 41 year old coal dealer with a wife and four children. 1st Lieutenant John Ryan had been wounded at Fredericksburg with a shell fragment wound near the liver. He had recovered and rejoined the company before Gettysburg. 2nd Lieutenant John Eagan's real name was Egan Lacey. He had joined the 69th as a private under a fake name to prevent contact with his relatives and had risen through the ranks and was also wounded at Glendale. Company F had five Sergeants and the roll was taken on July 3 by 1st Sergeant Robert Doak. The 5' 10" inch native of Donegal was married with two children. Sergeant George Mulholland was 39 and also from Donegal and also a veteran of the 24th Pa (Co A). He and his wife Isabella had four children. Sergeant John O'Neill was an unmarried 27-year-old machinist from Philadelphia. Sergeant John Gregg, age 24, was from Antrium, Ireland. Finally, 36 year old Thomas Kerr had been a veteran of US Military service both in the Mexican War and in the Florida Seminole Wars. The ranks of the men of Company F at the wall began with 5'10" Corporal Henry Thomas. The 34-year-old bachelor, who was the sole support of his mother, had been a bricklayer back in Philadelphia before the war. Private Patrick Harvey, age 50, like his brother and his nephew in company A, was tall and stood at the far right of the company line. Next to him would be James Hand, 40, native of Meagh, Ireland. Next in line was Private Peter Smith, a career soldier who had began as a corporal but was reduced in rank in January 1862. John McKenney, a stonecutter born in Ireland came next. 51 year old George Gilpin was to McKenney's left. He had been sick several months before the march north to Gettysburg and, at his age, would be frequently absent in hospitals during the war. Privates Joseph Dunbar and John Fullerton stood next in line and were tent mates for the first two years of the war. Nathaniel Laycock had been on furlough prior to Gettysburg but had rejoined the regiment. Privates Hugh Lynch and Charles Gallagher were both unmarried men who had widowed mothers back in Philadelphia depending upon their soldiers pay. In the center of the battle line stood Corporal David Haggerty, 32, and Private Patrick Condon, 36, respectfully. From Tyrone came Privates William Clark, 28, and from Dublin came Thomas Lindsay, 45. To their left were Privates Thomas Lafferty and John Dolan. Dolan, 52, was the oldest man in the company and a native of Sligo, Ireland, had been wounded at Antictam. The other Mulholland brother Arthur came next being the older brother at age 41. Neil McCafferty, 42, had a wife and three daughters back in Philadelphia. He had been "like a father to Sergeant Joseph Garrett of Company I. By his side was John Fleming, 33, born in Dublin and Patrick Rafferty, 42, a weaver before the war. Patrick Leister, who had a wife and two children, had been sickly during 1862 and had written his wife about the hardships of the march north after Lee. ". . . I am well after about 6 hard days march but we have about 80 miles more to go. I can't tell how manny died on the road . . ." The two shortest men in the company were Private Henry Allen, Tyrone born, who had joined the 69th late in 1862 and his tent mate Michael Gorman, a tailor before the war. At the far end of the line was Corporal Arthur McLaughlin a recently married cabinetmaker. That made 33 men ready for battle at the wall. The two men who were on detached service were drummer James Dickey, age 16, and Alexander Moore, age 46, with the hospital Corps.

The largest company was next along the wall to the left of Company F. Captain Patrick Tinen commanded the 41 men of Company D ready for action that morning. Tinen had a full compliment of 5 sergeants and 5 corporals plus two lieutenants to help him in the centre of the 69[ths] position. Patrick Tinen was a veteran both of the pre-war Philadelphia militia and of the 24th Pa. At age 28, he had risen through the ranks and was popular with the officers and the men of the regiment. 1st Lieutenant Charles McAnally born in Derry, was a man who enjoyed combat and often volunteered for skirmish duty. At 28, he had been a clerk before the war. McAnally had served at Fort Mifflin, Philadelphia with Captain James Harvey in 1861 and had been in Captain Thomas Smyth's Company H of the 24th Pa. 2nd Lt Michael Fay had been a tailor before the war and had been the Secretary of the "Meagher Guards" before the war and had begun his service in Company A of the 69th. First Sergeant James McCabe would take the roll on the morning of the 3rd. McCabe was recently married and was a close friend of 1st Lieutenant McAnally. Sergeant James Hand was married with two daughters and his wife Jane was to have a son a few weeks after Gettysburg. He was a native of Lowth, Ireland. From County Tyrone came Sergeant Francis Devlin who had been a soldier for most of the past 17 years. Finally Sergeant Jeremiah Gallagher from Donegal, 27, had a wife and a daughter back home.

Corporal Patrick Carney stood at the head of the battle line at 5'10". From Tyrone, Carney supported his widowed mother and had been sick during much of 1862. Private Owen Clark, 34, was next in line. At 6 foot tall he was the tent mate of James Costello. Private Costello had been wounded and captured at Antietam. Next in line was James Gallagher, Irish born and 25 years old. He would die in 1880 in a barroom brawl. Private John Nester,35, was from Phoenixville, Pa with four sons and a daughter. He had served in the 24th Pa and was alleged to have been in the 1st US Cavalry for two months in 1861.William McLean, 46, was the oldest an in the company and had been born in Scotland. Beside him stood Thomas Clark at 5'8" from Leitram, Ireland. He had worked in Danville, Pa in the Iron Mill before the war. Next came Private James McGinley a stone cutter who would later die in the 69's last battle of the war at Hatcher Run II. Beside him stood John Donavan, a cabinet maker from Cork, whose younger brother was the famous "Dynamite Donovan" of Irish fame. Patrick Coniff of Galway came next and had fought in every battle of the war thus far. Corporal Hugh Bradley was in the center of the company line. From Phoenixville, he had worked the iron mills both there and in Danville before the war. He was described as a "savage sort of fellow" by those who knew him and was the sole support for his mother back in Phoenixville, Pa. His mother was a widow with 9 children and who had sailed to American in 1843 after the death of her husband Bernard in 1841. Bradley had enlisted in the 69th at the age of 30 in August 1861."

James Duffy had been a Sergeant until the end of 1861 when he had been reduced to a private. He had been in company F of the 24th Pa and was born in County Donegal. Beside him was Peter Diamond of Derry, 37, was married with no children. His Captain Patrick Tinen called him a "brave soldier". From Cavan, Ireland came John Murray who immigrated by himself at age 17 to New York in 1854 and moved to Reading, Pa. Murray had publicly renounced all allegiance to the Queen of Great Britain in a public document in 1860. Private John McWilliams was born in Derry and had been with the 69th from the very beginning of the war. James Donahue, 44, was one of the older members of the company, a native of Tyrone, married and a weaver before the war. Beside him were Privates Charles Jenkins and James Elliot. Both were 27 years old with wives back home in Philadelphia. A 36-year-old Derry native, Charles McErland came next. McErland had been wounded in the right knee during the Peninsular campaign. He was a tent mate with Patrick Burns and John Haughey and after the war worked with them in railroad construction in Brazil, where he died. Corporal Patrick O'Conner, born in Cork, came next and beside him was the youngest man in the company James Donnelly at 19. He had started the war as the company drummer but became a member of the infantry in the spring of 1863. John Haughey, 37, from Tyrone was next in line, side by side with Private John Nellis who had been wounded in the Fredericksburg attack. Nellis, a bricklayer before the war, had joined the regiment in October 1862 after the Antietam battle. James McKenna, 42, was to the left of Nellis. The married baker from Frankford, Philadelphia had suffered from Rheumatism for most of the year. Francis McKee was a 36 year native of Armaugh, Ireland. Corporal Patrick Connelly, 24 from Tyrone had been promoted from private during the Peninsular Campaign. Private James McClosky was also from Tyrone and shared a tent with James Hennigan who had worked in the iron mill in Danville and had been wounded in the right knee at Antietam. Private James McCarty from Sligo had been AWOL in the sprig of 1863 but had returned to the regiment. William Hayes stood next. He had a widowed mother and one sister back home in Philadelphia. Patrick Burns, 32 from Managhan, Ireland, was another iron mill worker from Danville, Pa who had been recruited during the McAnally trip. The shortest private on the line was Charles Rogers born in County Tyrone and employed in Danville as an iron mill worker. Finally, at he very left end of the battle line was Corporal James McCann, also from Tyrone, who had been a weaver before the war began. Company D was indeed the largest company with 41 men on the line at the wall that morning. Company D had no detached soldiers and their drummer, Timothy Carr, was with the musicians prepared to do medical duties.

Company H to the left of D was the regiment's smallest company with only 20 men on the line July 3, 1863. The Company Commander, Captain Thomas Kelly, was on detached service back in Philadelphia as Quartermaster when the regiment left to move north after Lee in late June. The company was under the command of 1st Lieutenant Edward Thompson with First Sergeant Charles Williams. Thompson had been a member of the 24th Pa and had been in command of the company since Kelly's wounding at Antietam. From Waterford County, he had been wounded at Fredericksburg by a musket ball that entered his face beneath his right eye lodging in his neck. At Gettysburg he still carried the bullet which could not be removed. This caused him to be partially blind in the right eye. First Sergeant Charles was to take the roll and be second in command after the death of 2nd Lt Charles Kelly on July 2nd. Williams who was a carpenter before the war, had worked his way up from private during his three years of service. At 25, he supported his widowed mother. The Second Sgt was Jeremiah Boyle. He was married with four children at age 29. Sergeant David Shane had been a roofer and had risen from Private Sergeant since 1861. Sgts Dennis Laughery and Thomas Devin were both 22 year old men who worked as laborers and were born in Ireland.

The tallest Corporal, Frederick Murphy stood at the right wing of the company line. Having been born in Dublin, this 5" 10" former blacksmith stood at the edge of company D's left flank. Private Mathias Thomas, also 5'10" stood at the end with Murphy. After Gettysburg he would spend the remainder of his service time as a pioneer. Pioneers were a detached group of men responsible for tearing down fences, cutting trials and doing light engineering work at the Battalion level. Private Michael White, 24, came next, from Tipperary. Behind White stood Edward O'Brien, one of the oldest in the company at 41 a Canadian miner who had moved to Dansville before the war to work the mines there. Next in the front line, Thomas

McGrath had been captured at Antietam and had returned to camp just after the Fredericksburg battle. Behind him was Michael O'Hara a boatman before the war. The corporal inn the center was James Lynn, 20. Behind the corporal stood Robert Mellon who was the oldest man at age 42. He had been sick a number of times since joining the regiment in 1861. Anthony Angello, one of the few Italians in the regiment came next. He had been born in Venice and was a seaman before the war. He served as Captain Kelly's servant. Next, another boatman before the war, born in New York City, was Private James McCann. In front of him was a Welsh miner from the Pottsville mines named Daniel Miles. John Hurley was next in line. As a corporal, he had been sick during the Antietam campaign and had been sent to a hospital in Frederick. Maryland, from which he deserted in November 1862. He returned to the regiment that winter and was reduced in rank to private. A carpenter by trade, he had been detailed to a building crew early in the war. Next came Private Peter O'Conner who had joined the regiment in September 1862. He was born in Tyrone and had been a blacksmith before the war. At 5'5" and age 23 he was near the end of the battle line. At the very end of the battle line was Corporal John Cassidy, who still carried the Catholic prayer book over his heart which had helped deflect a bullet on the 2nd of July. Behind him, the shortest man in the company at 5'4", Private James Dolan, a blacksmith who had been born in Massachusetts. The detached men from Company H were all part of the teamster unit of the regiment. These men were with the wagon train parked down Taneytown Road near the location where the regiment had slept on the night of July 1. Head teamster John Rittenhouse had led five others. Rittenhouse had started as a driver and had been detailed as Assistant Regimental Wagon Master in May of 1862 and had been promoted to Head Wagon Master in October. James Murphy, 26, had been blacksmith before the war. The other blacksmith, Peter Conner, born in Tyrone was a 24-year-old blacksmith before the war. Conner may have fallen behind during the march because he was given a court martial hearing and fined $10 per month for three months for absence without leave in August. He seems to have caught up with the regiment sometime after the Gettysburg battle. He had suffered from kidney disease and rheumatism, which had developed after the battle of Fredericksburg back in the winter. The other team drivers included Privates Bartholomew Hart and John Harp both of whom had driven wagons from the beginning of the war and Chalky Gordon from Montgomery County, Pa 37. Drummer Hugh McGee, at 16, stood 5 foot one inch and joined the musicians on hospital duty.

Company C was the Color Company. In the center of the regiment, it would be charged with the protection of the national and the Green Irish battle flag of the 69th Pa. "The Emmett Guards" had been the most vocal of the Irish Nationalists in the regiment and had openly defied the orders of non-native Irish officers. This had led to and would led to further disciplinary issues both before and after Gettysburg. It's captain, James O'Reilly and its ranking lieutenant, John Connor, had resigned from the army in the month of April and brevet 1st Lieutenant Charles Fitzpatrick, age 27, was in command at Gettysburg. Fitzpatrick had been mustered as 2nd Lieutenant but had not yet received his papers as 1st Lieutenant by July 1. He had been wounded in the arm at Glendale. Second in command was Michael Dougherty who had been wounded both at Glendale and at Fredericksburg. This 25-year-old had been in the 24th Pa and became a 2nd Lieut. in April. The roll would be taken by First Sergeant William Coogan who had been with Company C of the 24th Pa. This 31 year old was born in Queens Ireland and had been a clerk before the war. Sergeant Michael Brady was one of the tallest men in a company of many tall men and had been selected to hold the National Colors on March 18, 1863. He was single and 27 years old. The Regimental colors were to be held by Sergeant David Kaniry native of Cork. A single man of 23 years, he and Brady would remain friends long after the war. He also had served in the 24th Pa company C.

At the head of the company line stood Corporal James Costello, 25, the tallest Corporal at 5"10" from Carlow County, Ireland. Costello was a veteran of the 24th Pa. Behind him was 5' 11' Private James Duff, born in Wicklow, Ireland in 1831. By Duff's side was 5' 10" John Prior native of Cavan. Prior was one of the newest members of the 69th, having only joined the unit in April 1863. This would be his first and last battle. Private Patrick Shields stood at the wall, a Tyrone born 35 year old. Beside him stood Donegal native, Andrew Cullen at 5' 9" who had been captured at Antietam and returned to the company in April. John Cronin was next in line. Kerry born, he had joined the regiment just before the Peninsular campaign. James Blakely was from Scotland and was the corporal in the center of the company. Before joining the 24th Pa in 1861 at age 35, he had been a weaver. Corporal Thomas Fagan at 5'9" was from Donegal and had been a baker before the war. Behind Blakely was John Campbell, a Tyrone native, age 35. At 5'9" Private John Ward who was born in Donegal, Ireland 38 years before stood at the wall. Beside Fagan, Private Thomas Supplee, 45, was one of the older men in the company and hailed from Limerick. It was on his parent's farm that the 24th had once trained. Private Michael Fahy, native of Mayo, had been wounded at Fredericksburg. His tent mate was Michael Toner, 29, a morocco dresser before the war. Frederick Funk, plumber before the war, stood at the wall and had been wounded at Glendale. A native of Flatbush, NY, Private James Thompson had moved to Montgomery County Pa and was employed as a stone cutter in a quarry before 1861. Corporal William Farrell, a 25-year-old Galway native, was next in line at the wall. Farrell had some problems with his regimental officers and would desert after Gettysburg and join the Marine Corps under the name "William Goblin". The next position was filled by Private Tim Lynch, also from Galway, and Farrell's tent mate. He had been a puddler at an iron rolling mill before the war. The final and shortest man in the company was 5" 5" Thomas Lundy, 45, the oldest man in the company. He had been a weaver before the war. Finally the corporal at he end of the line was Charles Dougherty the brother of the 2nd Lieutenant He would come through the Gettysburg battle unscathed but die in a Railroad accident in 1864. Four men were on detached service. The drummer, Charles Williams, and three men down at the hospital with the medical staff: Michael Welsh, John Ward and Patrick McGinchley. The small company would have 24 men at the wall.

Sergeant James McNamee of Company E took the roll that morning. Captain Thomas Wood had 28 men with him at the wall. Wood had taken command of the company after the murder of Captain McManus in April but had still not been officially mustered as Captain. Before the war, he had been a Cavan born carpenter and was 31 years old. His 1st Lieutenant John Devlin had been active in the Jackson Guards back in Philadelphia before the war and was a politically active Democrat. He had served in company E of the 24th Pa. Wounded and captured at Glendale, he had also been wounded at Antietam. At Gettysburg he was officially a 2nd Lieutenant but served as 1st Lieutenant 2nd Lieutenant John Taggart was missing that morning, down at the hospital. He had also served in the 24th and had been wounded at Antietam. Sergeant McNamee, who took the roll, would serve at the far end of the line that day in the corporal's position. He was born in Tyrone and was 23 years old. Sergeant Patrick Taggart was the older brother of the 2nd Lieutenant from the County Down. The other Sergeant was John Causey, 37, A former tailor from Philadelphia. Company E had a number of tall men who made up their right flank. The corporal who anchored that flank was Joseph McGarvey, 35, a prewar barkeeper from Donegal. McGarvey had been left behind at Camp Observation and did not rejoin the regiment until December of 1862. He would end the war as a Sergeant. Private Joseph Devlin at 5' 10" stood behind him. One of the three 42 year olds in the unit he had been sick during much of the war thus far and had been slightly wounded at Antietam. Next at the wall was Private Anthony Barnes from Sligo who had been involved in city government before the war. Private Thomas Gown had been a Corporal but was reduced in rank after Fredericksburg for cowardice during the battle. A Tyrone native, he would later become a teamster. 5' 10" Owen Slaugh, 36, came next. followed by Hugh Dornan, 42, a former weaver born in Derry. At the wall stood Private Hugh McAfee also from Derry and the tent mate of Slaugh. McAfee had been detached as a regimental cook several days before but joined his company for the battle. Behind him was Charles Gallagher, 22, from Donegal who after the battle would be detached to Battery F US Pa Artillery. Owen Carr, 37, from Tyrone, had been wounded at Antietam rejoined the unit in February. Beside him, and also wounded at Antietam, was Charles O'Neill, a lawyer by trade, also from Tyrone and Carr's long time friend. They were tent mates and would both be wounded again at Spotsylvania in 1864. The center of the line was anchored by Corporal Henry Cummings who was next in line to become a sergeant. To his left stood Thomas Flynn, born in Limerick who had been wounded in the foot at Glendale. He was a hotelkeeper and had served in the same militia company before the war with former Captain of Company B Thomas Fury. Flynn had severe problems with hemorrhoids on the march north. Flynn's tent mate by his side was John Clements of Derry who joined Charles Gallagher in the artillery after Gettysburg. John Smith was another of the 42-year-olds in Company E. Wounded in the face at Savage Station, he carried scars the rest of his life. Private John Sweeny, who served as Lieutenant Devlin's servant, was next in line. Then came Hugh Toner, 33, born in Donegal who had been a stonecutter before the war. Behind him stood Thomas McGrath from Tyrone. The youngest man in Company E was Private Hugh McKeever, from Donegal, who had joined the regiment in August 1862 and had been sick for much of his first year of service. Private John Doyle had been captured by the rebels at Snickers Gap, Va. in November 1862 and had returned in February. He was a weaver from England. Next came the Dougherty brothers from Derry, William and James. James was 22 with a young wife and child back home, and his brother William was a 20-year-old bachelor. At the far end of the line at 5' 4" were Privates Joseph McGinley and John Fee. Born in Donegal and Tyrone respectively, these men formed the end of the Company E line. Fee had been captured at Antietam. The three detached men from the company were 11 year old drummer Richard Fitzgerald, Teamster Owen Price and Ambulance Corp volunteer Henry Owen.

Company B, next to the left, had been the worst hit in the fighting the day before. It was down by 9 soldiers including it's commander from the day before, Lieutenant John McIlvane. The company Captain, John McHugh, was in Philadelphia recovering from an accidental gunshot wound to his knee. The company officers had been reduced during the spring in the political unrest in the regiment. The roll would be taken July 3 by Sgt David McCutcheon. Acting commander 2nd Lieutenant Murdock Campbell had still not been mustered and was officially still Sergeant Major of the regiment. Campbell had held a wide variety of positions in the regiment. At one time or another he had been Corporal, Orderly Sergeant, Sergeant Major, and would become 2nd and 1st Lieutenant He was a 30-year-old tailor born in County Clare. Sergeant McCutcheon was born in Tyrone and had been a bookkeeper before the war. He had been wounded in Fredericksburg where Company B also had high numbers of casualties. Sergeant John Britt had been a coach maker before the war. He was a 24-year-old veteran of the 24th Pa and a native of Westmeath Ireland. The third remaining Sergeant was Daniel McNichols, of Derry, who was a cordwainer before the war. To man the line there remained 4 corporals and 10 privates. The tallest Corporal was Aaron Rowe, 5' 9", a carriage maker from Newark, New Jersey. Rowe was a skilled marksman who was later detailed to the Brigade sharpshooter unit. Behind him stood 5' 10" Private John Farley, and beside Rowe was Mark Fitzpatrick from Galway. He had been sick on the march to Pennsylvania. George Campbell, 39, was born in Derry and was the oldest man in the company. Corporal Patrick McAnally, Tyrone born, stood next at the wall. He had been a Sergeant and had been sick during the Antietam campaign. He deserted from the hospital and, when he returned, he was reduced in rank to Corporal. Hugh Boyle, 35, was next, a native of Antrium Ireland. John Walls, 22, was the next Private at the wall with John Cain behind him, a watchmaker from Derry. The next Corporal was Edward McGuckin from Tyrone who had been a plasterer and was the brother of Andrew who had been wounded the day before and had died that morning. After helping bury his brother, Edward had returned to the wall. Behind him stood James Merrylees, at 5'5", who had been born in Vermont 24 years before and came to Philadelphia to join the Union army. Before the war he was a sheet metal worker. Arthur Hagen was next in line, a veteran of the 24th Pa. Behind him was Tyrone born weaver, Mark McCusker at age 28. The shortest man in the company at 5'3 ½" was Corporal Thomas Kearny at the end of the line. He was Tyrone born and a veteran of the 24yth Pa. Behind him in line was Private John Reagan, an unmarried native of Roscommon, Ireland who had been wounded at Antietam. Company B had a number of men detached on other service including Patrick McCartney and Patrick Todd with the Medical Corps as well as Joseph Cook and William Sullivan with the Brigade Commissary. Drummer Solomon Aarons, 17, was with the musician on medical duty. Company B would fight its second day of action with the smallest number of men at the wall—twenty three.

Captain William Davis—Company K

Gettysburg would be the only battle where Company K was not the flanking company and, as the roll was taken on July 3 by 1ˢᵗ Sergeant Josiah Jack, it must have been clear to all the men that they were not in the line of battle where they were used to being. Little did they realize that this change of positions would save many of their lives. Captain William Davis had been in command of the company since the beginning of its service in August 1861. That fact, and his previous service in the 69th New York National

Guard made him a favorite of many in the regiment. On the other hand he had served at the beginning of the war, not in the 24th Pa, but as a private in the 19th Pa. The Cork born 29 year old Davis would be entangled in much of the politics of the regiment.

Normally second in command of the company normally would have been 1st Lieutenant William Whildey, but he had been promoted to Adjutant of the regiment and was acting in that position. This then made 2nd Lieutenant John Johnson second in command. A native of Montgomery County Pennsylvania and a practicing Baptist, Johnson had served in Company K of the 17th Pa at the beginning of the war. 1st Sergeant Josiah Jack, taking the muster roll, was a 25-year-old dentist from Rochester, Pa. Company K had a full detail of 5 Sergeants and 6 Corporals. 2nd Sergeant Hugh Flooney was born in the County Down and had been a tailor before the war. He had been part of another company, which had been merged to form Company K in September 1861. 3rd Sergeant William Crout was a 30-year-old undertaker. Dennis Bradley had been wounded at Antietam. Finally Sergeant William Haskins had been promoted from Corporal in the spring and was a seaman before the war a native of New Bedford, Massachusetts. Isaac Van Zant was the tall corporal at the end of the line. A Quaker from Bucks County, Pa he had joined the unit in Feb 1862 at Harper's Ferry. He had acted as Hospital warden and as Regimental Commissary Sergeant over the past two months but was back in battle line this morning. Behind him in line was Patrick O'Connor, a 24 year old baker from County Louth, Ireland and 6 foot tall. From Derry, came Private Bernard Diamond. He was a blacksmith before the war. Next was Private Michael McCormick who had wounded in the leg at Fredericksburg. He had been born in Kildare, Ireland. John Dewson, a 23-year-old carpenter, stood in front of McCormick and was a native of Bridgeboro, New Jersey. To his right was John Haines, from the County Louth who, at age 27, was an engineer in civilian life. At the wall to his front was Joseph McIntosh, 18, a Philadelphia farmer before the war. Private John Buckley was next in line. He had been a lithographer before the war and was born in Manchester, England. He had been hit with two pieces of shell at the Battle of Antietam. The second Corporal was James Whitecar, at 5' 9", a former clerk. To his left were Private John McHugh and Corporal Joseph Vandersmith. McHugh, 22, had been a machinist before the war and VanderSmith, 32, had been an upholsterer. Private Patrick McShea, born in Caven Ireland was 36 years old and Private Francis Gleason, his tent mate was a 21-year-old Philadelphia tobacco salesman before the war. Next came Thomas Burns, 19, one of the youngest and in front of him one of the older men, Henry

Hughes, 36. 21 year old Henry Gevard had been captured at Savage Station and returned to the regiment just before Antietam where he was wounded. Josiah Bentz was a Private from Germantown, Pa. Thirty two, he had been a candy maker before the war. In front of him stood Corporal Robert Whittick a 19-year-old former news dealer who would be sick during much of the war. Moving to the left would be John Dugan,20, year old Philadelphia huckster and by him, Corporal Frank Butney. Philadelphia butcher Charles Shermer, 21. Shermer had been on leave in Philadelphia and returned just in time to march north. James Kelly stood in front of Shermer. He was a 21 year old Tyrone born moccocco dresser. The next pair at the wall was Privates John Simpson and Edward Morrisey, a bartender and a butcher before they joined the army. Next to them came the two shortest men of the company Private Jones and Corporal Lantz both age 20. William Jones was a former farmer from Camden, New Jersey. William Lantz had been a printer in Philadelphia in 1861. Finally, at the far left of the battle line behind Corporal Lantz, was Theodore Stratton,20, year a carpenter who had gotten sick during the Peninsular Campaign and was given a medical discharge. He returned to Philadelphia, recovered and returned to the regiment in May 1863, just in time for the Gettysburg campaign. The strength of Company K at the wall was 34 men. Only one soldier was on detached service at Gettysburg, Teamster Joseph Casey with the company wagon. The company's drummer was 17 year old Patrick Howe.

The far end of the regimental line was occupied by Company G, commanded officially by Captain Hugh Boyle. However Boyle's leg wound had made it necessary for him to ride in the company wagon on the march north and his over-activity on July 2 resulted in him being at the regimental hospital in the Frey barn on July 3rd. Command therefore passed to 1st Lieutenant Bernard Sherry. Company G had been the Montgomery Artillery, led by of James Harvey, and had largely gone into the 27th Pa at the start of the war. It was a unit with a strong "esprit de corps" and today would be in the maelstrom. Sherry had been wounded in the head at Savage Station by a fragment of shell. 2nd Lieutenant Michael Mullen had been wounded at Antietam. 30, he was unmarried and the sole support of his disabled parents. The five Sergeants of the company had all been together with the 27th Pa. First Sergeant Hugh Kelly took the roll that morning. A 30 year old painter from Tyrone, he had been First Sergeant for most of the war. James Walsh, from Dublin, was a weaver and had been sick during much of 1862. As one of the company's eldest men (47) he had been demoted in Dec 1862 but reinstated by Colonel O'Kane. Sergeants. John O'Conner and Michael McAller were

Private Thomas Burns—Company K

also from Tyrone, O'Conner, a blacksmith in 1861, and McAleer, a tanner. From Dublin, came John Wogan, 40, who had been sick in a hospital during most of 1862. The battle line of the company began with Corporal Cyrus O'Daniel, 23, a Philadelphia cabinetmaker. At 5' 11' he was at the right end of the ranks. Behind him stood 6' tall James Clay, 37 year old soldier from Doncgal. Beside O'Daniel was Private James Scinnader, 38, who had been wounded at Fredericksburg. Richard McErland, 5'10" from Derry, stood behind Scinnader. He was single and the sole support of his widowed mother. Privates Edward McCann and Michael Dooner were tent mates both 5' 9" and both 34 years old. James Coyle, 27, was born in Tyrone and had been in the 27th Pa at the start of the war. The next three men in line were a rarity for any Civil War company. The three Stinson brothers all were around 5' 8" tall and ranged in age from oldest brother John, who was 30, to Thomas, 26, to Robert, 25. All three had seen action in the war. Thomas Stinson, a bricklayer, who was active in Philadelphia Democratic politics, had been wounded and captured at Fredericksburg. Robert had been wounded at Antietam. All would survive the battle and the war. To their left were two privates, pre war laborers from Tyrone: Hugh Blakely and Hugh Donough. Next came William Smiley at the wall position, age 40 and behind him Patrick Lane from Tyrone age 27. The center Corporal was Patrick Noonan, 29, who had been wounded during the Peninsular campaign from Cork. Noonan had excellent penmanship and often wrote letters for the men of the company. Behind Noonan was Private Patrick Murphy, age 30. The next man in line Private Joseph Allen, from Derry, served as Hostler to Major Duffy during the Gettysburg campaign. 49, Allen was the oldest man in the unit. From Cork, Ireland came Cornelius Coakley and his tent mate Robert Hall an Englishman. To their left came Patrick Colgan of Tyrone, a shoemaker aged 28 and Private Alexander Middleton also age 28. To the left was Private James McEntyre, of Donegal, a married man with three children. Behind him stood John Blair, 30, from Derry, a plasterer before the war. James Bankin, 25, was a Private born in Philadelphia who had served in the 27th Pa as had his tent mate Bernard McManus. Next came Thomas McReynolds, 22, from Derry. At the very end of the company line and the regimental line were three men who would suffer in that exposed position. The brothers Laracy, Corporal James and Private Michael, were among the shortest men in the company. Born in Dublin, they had immigrated together to Philadelphia, and at age 30 and 31, had joined the 27th and the 69th together as well. Finally came Private James Rice, 20, son of Irish immigrants born in Philadelphia who at 5'4" would stand at the back and the end of the 69th Pa "Irish Volunteer" battle line. Company G would have 36 men ready for combat on July 3, 1863. Company G had contributed a number of men to the detached service of the medical and ambulance corps including Steve Boyle, William Fleming, Michael McCrea, and Thomas Scott. In addition, Private George Keen was a teamster with the wagon train.

CHAPTER FIVE

THE ATTACK

Like most summer mornings in Gettysburg Pennsylvania, morning on July 3, 1863 saw the temperature and the humidity rise with the sun. As the sun rose behind the Union lines, shadows of the trees behind the 69th Pa and the wall in their front stretched out across the fields toward the rebel lines. The darkness of the shadows covered the fields at their front where scores of bodies still lay from the fight the evening before. The breeze was slight and the odors of the decaying bodies of men in gray from Georgia were not yet a problem for the men lying at the wall. In a few hours, however, the sun would be overhead and there would be a need for blankets and tarps to be arranged to provide some shade from the heat, but not yet, as the shadows held the evening cool where the Lads from Erin rested. By afternoon, the temperature would rise to 87 degrees and the air would be warm and humid. The problem now, however, was food, not heat and as the men slept slouched against the wall where they had spent the night hunger was in their bellies. They had not been fed in any formal way since leaving Uniontown. Most of them had long since eaten any scraps of food they had packed away in their knapsacks, and all they had were hardtack and many had none of that. After all the days of marching and yesterdays fight, most of the men of the 69th slept soundly through the cool night. Many slept even more securely then usual surrounded by the extra rifles they had gathered from the field in front of their wall. Extra rifles that would give them a surprising level of firepower if the Confederate regiments again advanced upon them.

Those few men who had been awake at 4:00AM heard the shouts and saw the flashes along the skirmish lines to their right and left. It must have seemed odd to them that no Union skirmishers were directly in front of them that night. To the front and left out along the Emmitsburg Road four companies of the 19th Maine were stretched to the south of the Codori house. Those men not sleeping at that early hour saw several rebel cannons belonging to Parker's Battery fire at the Maine men and heard infantry skirmish fire in reply. In the far distance, rebel cannon occasionally threw shells at Little Roundtop. But the real action in the pre-dawn was to their front and south as skirmishers from the 14th Connecticut traded shots with Posey's rebel brigade. This action would build as both sides fed more and more men into the action. The Bliss house and barn had become an important location for rebel sharpshooters who were harassing the Union gunners on Cemetery Ridge. A location that had to be neutralized. But it was still pre-dawn and most of the men of the 69th slept through it all. There would be plenty of fireworks to come in daylight.

As the sun rose behind the ridge the men of the 69th were still in shadow. As they woke one by one they would ask men to their right and left who had been peering over the wall what was happening out to the front. The answer was easy. "Not much, some occasional cannon fire and some gunfire from the skirmish line" Some observant men would tell them about the growing action down to their right around the barn and house. Those awake could note that the evening before no man from the 69th was sent out to skirmish duty. The only movement beyond the wall by the "Irish Volunteers" was the scattered gathering of discarded rifles that lay across he field in front the wall. But in the dark dead bodies and the threat of rebel fire kept this to a minimum. There was no skirmish line directly in front of the 69th Around 7:00AM men from the 1st Delaware, from Hays Brigade, were sent out to the Bliss farm to chase away rebel sharpshooters who had been firing all morning in the dark toward Union lines. Some of the men of the 69th watched as about 30 men moved forward slowly across the Emmittsburg road and then out into the fields moving slowly toward the Bliss barn. Suddenly the rebels inside the barn opened fire and for a few minutes a firefight ranged. More Union troops approached and joined the action from the northern horizon. Suddenly, rebel cannons joined the fray booming their canister rounds toward the Union invaders. Occasionally, artillery rounds would sail toward Cushing's battery and strike somewhere on the ridge. General Henry Hunt, who was chief of Federal Artillery, rode up to Cushing and talked with him about helping out the attack on the Bliss farm. Cushing's crew began to prepare to open fire. Suddenly an explosion rocked the ridge to the right and rear of the 69th. A Confederate shell from Wyatt's Virginia gunners had found its mark, landing in the just opened lid to the ammunition chest on Limber #2. The explosion would be the first violent flash of noise and light that would later dominate the ridge that day. Those in the 69th still sleeping jolted awake to the roar of ammunition exploding, not only from Limber number two but from the limbers on each side. The tremendous explosion hurled men and horses into the air. Flames and pieces of wood were everywhere. The men of the 71st Pa, who were nearest the explosion, were covered with wooden slivers and smoke. The horses of guns one, two and three panicked and tried to break free and run. The first sight for many men of the 69th that morning was the entire team of horses from gun number one jumping the wall at the void to their right and rushing down the hill toward Emmitsburg road. Then the heads of the men of Erin shifted forward. From across the valley came the shouts and yells of the rebel gunners who had witnesses their direct hit. This morning, it was clear, the Confederate army was across that valley primed for battle.

With every man in the 69th Pa as an audience, Cushing's guns went into action. It was now about 8:00 am and Paddy Owen's regulars would closely observe the first artillery duel of the morning. The six guns of Cushing's battery began firing at the two rebel batteries that had advanced to deal with the Bliss Farm combat. Each time Union gunners found their mark, the lads would send up a cheer from the front wall. Each time a rebel shell would fly overhead, they would duck and cringe behind that wall.

Now awake to a man, these men of the 69th Pa looked to their right and to their left to see which other regiments had joined them at the wall. To their left, sloping downhill along the wall continuation were four companies of the 59th NY. The 59th had suffered such losses at Fredericksburg and Chancellorsville that they had been reduced from a 10-company regiment to a 4-company battalion with about 145 men. The day before, they had lost heavily. Hit head on by the 48th and 3rd Georgia, they lost their commander, Lieutenant Col. Max Thoman and at least 4 others killed plus 9 others wounded and out of action. During the bombardment to come, they would lose another dozen to shellfire. The men of the 69th were well aware of the heavy losses within the 59th NY on the 2nd and had heard the rumors of the court martial and arrest of their old commander and the resignation of many of their officers over the past two months. They must have wondered how well the 59th would hold if the rebels attacked in force again. To the left of the 59th NY was the 7th Michigan, the men who had first crossed the Rappahannock to drive the rebels from the streets of Fredericksburg last December. They were a tough unit that could be counted on.

When they glanced to their right, the lads of the 69th saw only open space. The 55 yards to the right of Company I were empty, open space that gave an uneasy feeling to the men on the right companies I, A, F and D. To make things worse this emptiness overlooked their position because the ridge which they defended ran downhill from north to south as much as it dropped downhill from east to west. They must have wondered, "who will defend our right if the Confederates attack us?" The reason for the void at present was clear as they looked to their right and rear and saw the six rifled cannon of Cushing's battery drawn up in order along the crest of the hill. No men occupied the 55 yards in front of Cushing so as to provide a clear field of fire for his cannon. But would a regiment be brought forward to guard this void when the rebel infantry advanced?

To the rear lay the rest of the Philadelphia brigade: The Seventy-Second behind the copse of tress in reserve, the Seventy-First to the rear and right along the crest line, and two companies of the 106th to the left of the 72nd Pa directly behind the left companies of the 69th.

The ten companies lay along the wall. The wall sloped downward so that Companies I and A on the far right looked downhill at the middle of the line and at far off companies G, K and B. Company G was still out of the regular battlefront order as they had been the day before. But there they would stay, for the first time being the left flank company. From the rear near the dirt road at the crest, it appeared that the entire 69th regiment was down in a gully with trees behind them and rising earth at their right and rear. The men behind that wall had done what they could to prepare it as a defensive works. Many of the smaller trees and scrubs in the copse had been cut down and the wood used to make protection for firing. When the 69th had arrived some of the wall still had rail on top to deter cattle from crossing. The newly cut wood would expand that and provide cover for heads and eyes to peer across the valley 1. The men know that theer had been losses from the evening before when they fought the Georgians, but morning muster would formalize the numbers and all would know who was ready for this day's work—company by company. The First Sergeants began the daily morning routine. The Sergeants would check the lists and history would record the presence of each of this band of brothers who would fight this day.

The Field Officers huddled together where they had spent the night on the ground to the left of the copse of trees, with a small fire to heat some coffee. Colonel O'Kane, pipe in hand, prepared to start the day. Lieutenant Colonel Tschudy, his head bandaged from the wound received July 2, had already made his mind up about staying at the front with the men. His wound could wait another day for better care. With them was Major Duffy who was not as close personally with the two senior officers. He was 27 years old and they almost 40, both born in 1824. Duffy had, as Captain of Company A back in January, asserted that he was the senior Captain of the regiment and therefore entitled to the open Major position, a position that went to Tschudy instead in March. In February, Tschudy had written to the Governor and contradicted Duffy's assertions and had gotten the support of both Owen and O'Kane for the position. James Duffy who related well with most of the Irish nationalists in the regiment never was close with Owen or O'Kane and Tschudy.

Along with O'Kane and Tschudy was Adjutant William Whildey. Whildey had been appointed May 1 but would not be mustered until July 16. Never-the-less, at age 29 he would serve as regimental adjutant at Gettysburg. A protégée of William Davis, Captain of Company K, Whildey had risen from Sergeant to 2nd Lieutenant and then 1st Lieutenant and had shown considerable battlefield bravery during the Peninsular campaign. He was a bachelor who provided the sole support for his mother in Philadelphia who had been abandoned by his father before the war.

Finally in the group of Field Staff around the fire was acting Sergeant Major Thomas Norman. Norman was still one of the most unsettled men in the regiment with regard to his rank position. On the morning of July 3rd he was still being paid as a Corporal of Company A, although he was carrying out the duties of Sergeant Major. Norman had experienced, more than any man in the regiment, the topsy turvey rules of mustering and commission in the Union army. His rise from private and Adjutant clerk to Corporal had had been followed by his promotion to Sergeant Major on June 6th 63. However, because the promotion of the previous Sergeant Major, Murdock Campbell, to 2nd Lieutenant had never been officially approved, Norman was still mustered as Corporal Co A. To make things more complicated he had also received an appointment as 2nd Lieutenant himself the day before, June 5, but never commissioned because of the regiments low numbers. Norman would serve in this battle as the acting Sergeant Major.

Sometime during the morning it is probable that several other field Staff would have moved forward to the front lines from their rear positions. The regimental medical officers had set up a base of operations in the Peter Frey House just on the other side of the ridge down by Taneytown road. Surgeon Burmeister and Assistant Surgeon McNeil had dealt with the regiment's dying and wounded from the fighting the day before and would have moved up to the wall to report to Col. O'Kane before returning to their field station where a dozen men had been detached to them for the coming fight. Burmeister's report confirmed the losses from the fight with Wright's Georgia brigade as 9 killed and 10 wounded and off the front line. Several men such as Tschudy and Whildey and about 5 enlisted men who were slightly wounded but made the choice to stay at the wall.

Morning muster would continue . . . .

As morning muster was completed, history would record those exactly 292 men of the 69th Pa "Irish Volunteers" would be at the wall on Friday July 3, 1863. The morning would develop much the same as the first half of the day before: the 69th Pa at the front of the Philadelphia brigade almost like sitting in the balcony of a theatre watching the play begin to open. The first act would begin with skirmishing and fighting to their front and left around a house and barn belonging to William Bliss and would be punctuated by a few rounds of artillery fire from each side. Occasionally the attention of the lads would be turned to the front and south where sporadic skirmishing would occur. Unlike yesterday's balcony observation there would be no passive observation of a massive battle to their front and south. The men would have plenty of time this morning to sit and think and prepare for whatever the rebels had planned for them. For these 6 hours of morning, when they weren't watching the stage out front, they would be dealing with the rising heat and the gnawing feeling of hunger in their bellies. Small fires heated the last scraps of food that had been made into a stew and boiled coffee that helped wake up the men.

By 9:00 am, the time had come for the 69th to join the action. Muster calls were over and while most of the men remained at the wall and prepared for the day. A skirmish detail was organized which would include some men of the 69th. Captain James Lynch of the 106th was detailed to lead a group of about 125 men forward to fill in the space at the front that had never been occupied the night before by Union pickets. The detail would include some men from Companies A and B of the 106th Pa, some men from companies A and K of the 72nd and a detail of men from the 69th. In the fighting the day before, Companies A & B of the 106th Pa had been on picket duty after the Wright attack and had returned to gather ammunition down by the Taneytown road. When they returned to their regiments position behind the crest they discovered that the other eight companies of their regiment were gone. They had been sent to help out General Howard on Cemetery Hill. These two companies spent the night in position behind the copse of trees. They would not see their comrades from Companies C through K again until the evening of July 3rd. Captain James Lynch, commander of the skirmish line that morning, made it clear years later that he did not take out all of Companies A & B. "General Webb sent me at about eight or nine o'clock in the morning to take charge of the skirmish line, assisted by the details of two companies of the Seventy-second, and the details were made from the different companies of the Sixty-ninth and One Hundred and Sixth that were out there. I was in command of the details but I did not have my company with me. The two companies were not in the skirmish line on the third day. When the cannonade commenced I was on the skirmish line and all this took place over our heads and we were very glad of it." The 125 men under his command would be from companies D & K of the 72nd (about 90 men) and about 15 each from the 106th and 69th. Commanding the men from the 69th Pa was 1st Lieutenant Charles McAnally from company D. The other men with him would possibly be Corporal Farrell McGovern of Co A, Privates Owen Clark, James Elliot and James Donohue of his own company, plus several others.

1ST Lieutenant Charles McAnally—Company D

As McAnally's small band moved out to the Emmittsburg Road, they moved to the left of the 106th and 72nd and took up a location first directly to the right of the Codori House and then moved outward to the first hill in the fields beyond the road. These dozen men with McAnally pushed out farther than the rest of the Union skirmish line. Lynch explained the McAnally position, "The Sixty-ninth detail had gone over to the line of the Bliss House, to the position occupied the day before and they fell back to the advance guards, just to the crest of the hill, beyond the Emmittsburg Road and I brought up the reserve".

As the men at the wall watched a dozen or so of their comrades go out to the Emmittsburg Road and beyond, another scene unfolded for their view. Off to the right another attempt to chase the rebel sharpshooters from the Bliss properties began. Even as the Philadelphia Brigade skirmish line was taking form, 200 men from the 12th New Jersey, under the command of Captain Richard Thompson, moved forward to the Bliss barn building. The men from New Jersey seized the barn and chased away the Confederates but soon a counterattack developed with a rebel artillery battery firing shells into the captured barn. Now it was time for the New Jersey men to retreat back to their own lines. Once again rebel sharpshooters fired upon the Union artillery batteries on the ridge. Soon things quieted down and the men of the 69th could turn their attention to other matters. There was the issue of food. There was none for 48 hours now. The men saw the sun begin to move up over the tree and scrub line the shadows disappeared and the day got hotter and more humid. Private John Buckley remembered one activity that took up the men's time. "We abstracted the buckshot from the ammunition and reloaded the spare guns putting 12 to the load and almost every, man had from two to five guns loaded that were not used until Pickett got within fifty yards of the wall." 2 Many men spent the morning as they had the evening before lying against the wall reloading the spare guns in the manner described by Buckley. Most of the 69th was by now armed with Springfields and Enfields but not all. The ordinance report for April 1863 shows that companies C, D, F & H still had a number of men armed with .69 cal. rifled muskets capable of firing Buck and Ball shot. Company F, for example, all were armed with .69 cal rifles. In fact, ammunition inventories in April show companies D, E & H still carrying buck and ball rounds. More importantly almost all the men at the wall that morning had excellent knowledge of the use of the .69 cal rifles they has gathered from the field since almost all of them had used these types of rifles during the Peninsular campaign. About 300 extra rifles were now in the possession of the 69th Pa for use in the coming battle. **3**

This was also the time to build crude shelters from the sun. Many men fixed their bayonets and stuck their rifles into the ground to use as poles for blankets to be stretched to provide shade. Others used sticks and rail to construct shelter from the now blazing sunshine. Some in the 69th watched from the wall, as the final attempt occurred to clear the rebels from the Bliss House and Barn, an attempt that would create brief artillery duel all around the men of the 69t[h.] At about 11:00AM approximately 60 men from the 14th Connecticut were sent out to the Bliss properties. This time they had an order to burn the house and barn to the ground and once and for all end the protection used by the rebel sharpshooters. Out they charged and Confederates again abandoned the shelters. The rest of the 14th Connecticut followed and occupied the buildings. Confederate artillery opened up on the barn and a brief artillery duel began between McCarty's and Wyatt's Confederate gunners who were blasting away at the barn and the batteries of Arnold, Cushing, Brown and Rorty who were undertaking counter battery fire. Lasting only ten minutes, this fire from the guns to the right and left of the copse of trees would pinpoint for the entire Confederate artillery line the exact location of the 4 Union batteries at the center of the line.

The lads of the 69th knew they were well protected by artillery. To their rear and right was the six gun battery of Lieutenant Alonzo Cushing (Battery A 4th US Artillery) and beyond them behind the rear stone wall another six guns belonging to Captain William Arnold (Battery A 1st Rhode Island Artillery). To the rear and left were two more batteries. Behind their left wing companies were the 4 guns of Lieutenant T. Fred Brown (Battery B 1st Rhode Island Artillery) and beyond that 4 10 lb. Parrotts under Captain James Rorty (Battery B 1st New York Artillery. Rorty was a commander well known to many in the 69th. He was active in the Fenian movement and well respected by the Irish soldiers throughout the army. Once again, the men of the 69th Pa had been spectators to the entire engagement. Noon was near and quiet settled over the entire field. It was a time for dozing in the sun but off to the north came the smell of food and all down the line men looked to see the crews of Cushing's batteries preparing lunch. The artillery had rations and began cooking them.

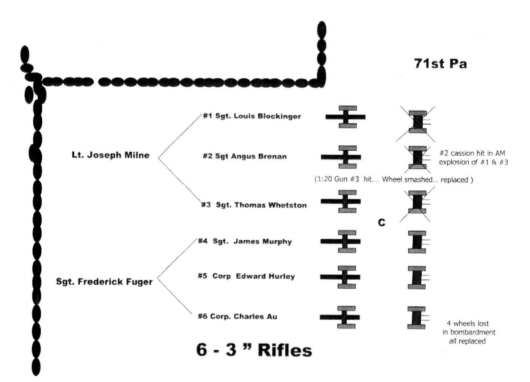

Cushing at the Angle 1:07-2:30

Cushing's Battery Position

Others in the regiment remembered the relative quiet and the hunger of noontime. Private Anthony McDermott at the far right of the line was in position to look down the entire length of the 69th's companies. He wrote, "The morning of the third passed off quietly except the usual picket firing, sometimes very brisk and again all quiet until about noon. The troops had all finished eating their stew, or sipping their coffee, when a death like stillness prevailed throughout the Army, the sun was shining in all its glory, giving forth a heat almost stifling and not a breath of air came to cause the slightest quiver to the most delicate leaf or blade of grass. Of that stillness you have often heard, no language of mine could cause you to imagine its reality, such a stillness I had never before experienced, nor since, and I have borne part in every engagement of the Army of the Potomac." 4

Watching the Cushing crews prepare their coffee fires and begin cooking a midday meal proved too much for some of the men and they shouted back at the canoneers to see if they could spare any food for the men at the wall. In the center of the 69th line with Company E was Private Joseph McKeever and McKeever was hungry. He had joined the regiment later than many of his comrade's back in August of 1862. McKeever had been born in Ireland and immigrated to Philadelphia with his mother Mary. He had finally persuaded her to give him permission to join the "Irish 69th" in the summer of 1862 and she had signed the minor consent form on August 18th. Hugh, who later after the war called himself Joseph, was a short nineteen-year-old who was often sick. He was ill at Harper's Ferry in the fall of 1862 after joining the regiment and missed the Fredericksburg battle. He rejoined the regiment Jan 25, 1863 but missed many months of 1864 again sick in a hospital. However he must have been impressive when he was in camp because he rose from Private to Corporal to Sergeant by the end of the war. On the morning of July 3 around noon, this impressive, short and hungry private decided to take action. McKeever liked to wear an old Kossuth hat, which was useful for gathering provisions. Looking over to the location of Cushing's battery, McKeever saw that they had just unloaded several boxes of hardtack so he left his position on the wall and walked over to the artillerymen to ask if he could have some crackers for his comrades. Cushing's men must have agreed because McKeever took off his floppy hat, broke open one the boxes of hardtack and began filling up. With little rations for 48 hours, company E and all others who could share in his bounty would welcome his return. Just as he filled his hat to the brim, a cannon fired across the valley and then an explosion of rebel artillery followed. McKeever with his hat overflowing with hardtack crackers rushed back to his company and the bombardment of July 3rd was on. McKeever told his story years later "Just before that, while the stillness was going on, this one point I remember, Cushing's Battery served out rations and I had an old Kossuth hat; we had little or no rations for forty-eight hours and I got one box and dumped it into this old Kossuth hat and as I was doing that the first signal or gun was fired right in our immediate front and then the whole of the batteries opened. The cannoneers and the men of the battery were called to their position and I ran down to the front and it was on the right of my regiment and Owen (sic) came and called to me to go to my place ad I had to run below the colors to get where I was." 5

Private McDermott years later spoke of the few moments before the opening of the cannonade. "About noon a stillness that was deathlike and unusual at such a time, an anxious look could plainly be seen on the faces of the men and feelings of mingled dread and determination pervaded the minds of all—a harbinger of the coming storm that was to cover the fields with so much blood drawn from patriot as well as from the traitor." 6

The signal gun fired from the Washington Artillery in the Peach Orchard began the most massive artillery duel ever engaged on American soil. The men of the 69th who had felt secure to have four artillery batteries surrounding them now realized that thee same four batteries would be the target of focus for the entire Confederate cannon line. Within moments hundreds of solid shot, exploding shells and wooden splinters and rocks filled the air and ricocheted into every location. The Brigade historian wrote, "Then at intervals along the entire line solitary shots were fired, as if intended for signal guns in preparation. These were quickly followed by others and in a few moments there burst forth from the whole Confederate line a most terrific fire of artillery. One hundred and twenty guns concentrated their fire on that portion of Meade's position held by the Second Division, Second Corps. Shell, round shot, Whitworth bolts and spherical cases were flying over and exploding about us at the same time. Almost every second, ten of these missiles were in the air; each as it went speeding on its message of death, indicating its form by a particular sound. The shrieking of shells or the heavy thud of round shot were easily distinguished from the rotary whizzing of the Whitworth bolt.

When these agents of destruction commenced their horrid work, no portion of the line, from the front to a point far in the rear of the Taneytown road, afforded any protection against their fury. Men who had been struck while serving the guns and were limping towards the hospital, were frequently wounded again before they had gone a hundred yards." 7

Private Robert Whittick near the colors noted "After the cannonading began, we were all hugging the earth and we would have liked to get into it if we could" **8** Private McDermott in Company I had the very best vantage point to see the impact on the position of the 69th companies. With his company at the highest level of the line he could, look down the line and view all. "At 1 o'clock the stillness was broken by the discharge of one gun from the enemies lines—the right of Longstreet's position—The men start all gaze toward the Confederate positions at the same time moving quickly to their posts, again the air is disturbed by a sound or rather many sounds almost in one, as a volley of Artillery pours out deafening roar. The air is filed with whirling shrieking hissing sounds of solid shot and the bursting shells. All ands throw themselves flat upon the ground behind the stone wall. Nearly 150 guns belch forth messengers of destruction sometimes in volleys, again in irregular but continuous sounds traveling through the air high above us or striking the ground in front ricocheting over us to be embedded in some object to the rear, others strike the wall scattering stones around. The fire of those batteries seems to be concentrated on Cemetery Ridge part of which was held by our regiment." **9**

The fire of the Confederate guns had two goals; both to silence the Union artillery and to drive off the Union infantry. The poor quality of the Confederate fuses on exploding ammunition (spherical shot) would bring failure to both goals.

Many historians have noted that an estimated failure rate of 70% of the rebel fuses would mean that a large amount of ordinance would fly over the heads both of the gunners and infantry alike. reducing the rain of iron pouring down upon them. But the solid shot and those fuses that did work brought destruction upon the ranks of the 69th Pennsylvania nevertheless. Lee's overall purpose was to recreate the classic Napoleonic massive assault that was based upon massive artillery fire to a single point in the enemy line followed by massive infantry attack to break the center.

At some point during the bombardment. John Harvey Jr. at the far end of the Company A line was struck in the right side of the head by a piece of shell fragment. He was cared for by his father John Harvey Sr. by 1st Sergeant Ralph Rickaby and Corp Patrick Moran. His head was wrapped, and he drifted in and out of consciousness as the attack continued. In the same company, Private Thomas Standing caught a shell fragment in his left leg, possibly from the same exploding shell that wounded Harvey Jr. and was probably helped by his tent mate Bartholomew Conway. The Frankfort, Philadelphia carpenter stayed at the wall and was later during the fighting able to move back toward the copse of trees. In company I at the right wing a shell fragment hit Tom Divers in the head and killed him. Further down the line. a piece of shell fragment flew through the air and hit Private John Dolan of company F in the small of the back on his right side. He may have lain at the wall during the rest of the fighting, or perhaps was helped to the rear by comrades. In the middle of the regimental line with company, H Private Thomas McGrath was wounded by an exploding shell, which ripped a large chuck of flesh from his left hip. He had been captured at Antietam and returned Dec 16th just in time to participate in the Fredericksburg assault. McGrath never recovered from his shell wound and was discharged from the service on March 29, 1864 after being in Finley Hospital for eight months. McGrath's wound knocked him out of action as the fighting swirled around him and probably required the attention of his Corporal, Frederick Murphy, to deal with the loss of blood from the wound.

At least one exploding shell landed right in the midst of the center of the 69th during the bombardment. Private Thomas Supplee, age 42, of Company C (the flag company) was lying behind the wall when a shell exploded near him burning off his shoes and severely damaging both feet. This painful wound required treatment with iodine until August 22 at the General hospital in Philadelphia. Supplee had trouble walking long after the battle. His corporal, James Blakely, probably watched over him as he lay on the ground behind the wall during the coming fight. Corporal James Costello, also in Company C, lost two fingers from his right hand when a shell fragment flew by him at the wall. His index and middle finger would have to be surgically removed after the fight. 25 year old Private Thomas Flynn in Company E had been wounded in the Peninsular campaign and received a shell fragments in the left shoulder during the cannonade and was disabled from further combat. He was hospitalized at South Street hospital in Philadelphia and then discharged in September. Also in company E was Private Hugh Dornan who received a piece of shell in his right leg but was able to continue firing at the wall position. He was sent to Germantown Hospital in Philadelphia after the battle where he deserted and then returned to join the Veteran Reserve Corps in November of 1863. There is reason to believe that it was the same shell that exploded behind companies E & C that was responsible for the wounds of Supplee, Flynn and Dornan. Perhaps that shell also tore into the Captain of Company E, Thomas Wood, whose right side midway between the hip and arm was ripped open by a sharp fragment of shell. The metal tore flesh from his side and ripped the muscles of the chest. It is probable that he was evacuated during the bombardment along with Private Flynn due to the nature of their wounds. A piece of shell fragment hit Corporal Patrick O'Connor (Co D) in his right foot lodging in his ankle as he lay against the wall during the cannonade. O'Connor would spend a few months in a Chestnut Hill, Philadelphia hospital and then desert, never to be heard from again.

Over at the wall came another casualty of the bombardment from Company C. Private John Prior was struck on the head by a piece of rail that had been hit with a solid shot. He was knocked senseless and suffered headaches for weeks after the battle while hospitalized in Baltimore. In the front middle of Company C Corporal Henry Cummings suffered a concussion sometime during the fight which ended his service in the 69th after many months in a hospital. One of the most tragic casualties was psychological, As Private Charles McErlain (Co D) sought protection from the bombardment against the wall, he suddenly had what modern doctors would call a nervous breakdown or "shell shock". His comrade Peter McAnanny stated that "he became insane from the firing of Artillery". Another comrade by him at the wall, Francis McKee, stated "he acted very strange afterwards and was sent to the Insane Asylum". For Charles McErlain the war was over and he never recovered mentally.

McErlane's good friend Patrick Burns would suffer headaches for weeks after the battle. Off to the left, in Company K, Sergeant Dennis Bradley took a small piece of shell fragment in his breast but continued his duty behind the company.

Four different soldiers in Company G at the end of the battle line of the 69th had injuries caused by cannon fire. Of these two certainly were caused by the "friendly fire of Cowan's battery which fired canister directly over the company well after the infantry attack began. However the Laracy brothers each suffered shell fragment wounds which could have occurred during the bombardment. Corporal James Lacey, who had been a prisoner after Savage Station, took a hit by a jagged piece of shrapnel that tore a piece of flesh three inches log, two inches wide and an inch and a half deep into his left shoulder blade region. It is uncertain when this occurred but it clearly knocked him out of the fighting with a large loss of blood. He lay upon the field for a considerable time after the battle ended. This injury ended his military service being discharged Feb 18 of 1864 for the injury. His brother Michael, a private in the same company (G) received a fragment wound on the right side of his head behind the ear which caused him deafness in the right ear for the rest of his life. He would spend time in Chestnut Hill hospital until late November 1863 when he would return to his unit and served the rest of the war as a private. Sixteen, and possibly eighteen members of the 69th Pa were casualties of the bombardment.

The shells from the rebel guns also flew toward the 69th medical staff that was located at the Peter Frey Farm down the east slope of the ridge alongside the Taneytown road. The medical staff had been busy all morning with the care of the men who had been wounded in the July 2 fighting. Located in the red barn and white farmhouse along with Surgeon Frederick Burmeister and Assistant Surgeon Bernard McNeill, was hospital Stewart Richard Schofield. Schofield would coordinate the work of the 69th men detailed to the regimental hospital including Privates Patrick Todd (B), John Ward (C), Henry Owens (E), Alexander Moore (F), and Henry Schwartz (G). In addition the ten musicians of the regiment had already been pulled back to the regimental hospital. They had carried the killed and wounded back to the rear lines after the July 2 fight and would be ready to go to work again today when the enemy attacked. Attached to help with the Ambulance corps were several men from the 69th including Patrick McCarthy (B) Michael McCrea (G) and Thomas Scott (G).

While shells exploded and bounced through the Frey property, the medical unit was busy taking care of the wounded from Wright's attack. Soon newly wounded from the cannonade would be arriving. In the field beside the Frey Barn, were newly dug graves for 2nd Lieutenant Charles Kelly, Captain Michael Duffy, Sergeant James McShea as well as Privates O'Neill, Gallagher, Todd, and Harrington. Each body had been wrapped in an army blanket and a wooden board with each name placed at the head the grave. Many others would follow these 7 new graves by the end of the day. Sgt James McShea's good friend, Sergeant John Britt probably helped bury him and wrote later to his wife of the death. Inside the barn, the most seriously wounded included Private Andrew McGuckin (B) who was shot in the chest the day before and would die before evening. Private James McNulty needed careful attention and would die July 6th of his chest wounds. Private Luke Mealy (B) who had a bullet wound in his hand was still missing. Steve Sullivan, company D, had a bullet in his right arm. Private William Hackett (K) still did not know if he would lose his right arm and Private Francis McGill (B) feared that the bullet that tore into his upper arm would result in amputation. Sergeant Patrick Kelly (Co D) had a shell fragment in his right shoulder that could have, but did not, result in amputation. Knocked out of action and requiring close care was 1st Lieutenant John McIlvain (B) with a bullet in his upper right arm and one of his Sergeants, Nicholas Farrell, who required surgical help to pick several fragments of buckshot out of his right leg. Farrell's left leg had been hit with a bullet at Fredericksburg. Private William McNichol (K) was semi conscious with a skull fracture that would require several pieces of skull being removed. Finally Patrick Noonan from Company G had a bullet lodged in his left breast that caused concern and had to be removed from two inches below behind the left nipple.

Fortunately, no shells hit the barn although the sounds of the bombardment must have made the experience of those inside a living hell. Also, back at the hospital during the bombardment was Captain Hugh Boyle of Company G. Boyle had come down with dysentery and was suffering from recurrence of pain and an abcess in his left thigh from the bullet wound he received at Antietam. He had been unhealthy for quite a while and may have ridden in the company wagon on the march north. Boyle's bad luck started at the construction of Fort Ethan Allen in 1861where he was struck accidentally by a pick in the left hip and later during the building of the Grapevine Bridge across the Chickahominy in 1862 where his hand was crushed by some rolling logs. His thigh wound at Antietam never really healed.

Back at the front, the real brunt of the rebel cannonade fell on the artillery batteries that surrounded the 69th Pa. McDermott wrote "Our batteries reply. Battery A Lieutenant Cushing & Brown's R.I. Battery occupy the crest of the ridge to our rear. Together with the batteries on the Round tops, Old Cemetery: Cemetery and Culp's Hill but ere long Cushings and Brown's are almost completely silenced their guns shattered into splinters, horses disemboweled, their flesh and entrails scattered, men beheaded, limbs torn and bodies most horribly mangled into shapeless and un recognizable masses of human flesh, at last after nearly two hours, the fire slackens, almost ceases." **10**

The statistics tell the story of the destruction of the batteries that supported the 69th. To the right and behind the rear wall lay the battery of six guns of Arnold. One by one the gunners of his battery were put out of action. Gun #1 collapsed on its side with a smashed wheel. In Cushing's battery a caisson was hit and exploded detonating the caisson beside it. Gun # 3 lost its wheel and required a replacement. Off to the rear and left of the 69th Brown's 1st Rhode Island with 4 12lb Napoleons, which had been the target of Wrights attack the day before, lost gun #4 when a round got stuck in Gun #4. Just slightly to the South, the Battery of Rorty (the 1st New York Light) had lost two of its four Parrot rifles and most of its caissons.

Before the cannonade ended Cushing would lose two of his guns (Numbers 2 & 6) and would ask for and receive permission to move the four remaining 3" rifles down toward the wall. This he and his crews did and the four guns continued to fire.

Suddenly a cease-fire was called for the Union gunners. A quick survey convinced Brigadier General Henry Hunt, Union artillery commander that it was time to pull the four batteries surrounding the 69th and replace them with new guns. Brown's and Arnold remaining guns were limbered up to leave the field but Cushing independently decided to keep his two remaining guns (#4 & #5) in action. Rorty was now dead and as Brown's guns were limbered up to be withdrawn Lieutenant Robert Rogers ordered the two remaining Parrots to be pushed down toward the front. One of which was soon overloaded and exploded. New Batteries would be arriving to replace those destroyed and withdrawn.

How long did the cannonade last ? McDermott suggests that the bombardment lasted nearly two hours. But elsewhere he states "It lasted, I should judge, between one and two hours". (1889 72nd Trial). Others gave a variety of estimates. Joseph McKeever, Private Co E, testified that it lasted for "one hour or more", Also in Company E was Private Robert Whittick who saw it this way . . . "When they opened artillery on us in the morning, they ordered us to lay down. We laid there I suppose until one or two o'clock, somewheres there and then they advanced in three lines on us". The Brigade historian, Charles Banes, figured that the whole bombardment went for one hour and 45 minutes. The memories of the men vary ranging from a little over 2 hours to a little under one hour. The best available estimate based upon all data is that the rebel cannonade began at slightly past 1:00 and ended around 2:20PM. Off to the right with Company I, Sergeant Joseph Garrett recalled "abut an hour and a half, I suppose".

Somewhere in the later moments of the cannonade general Winfield Scott Hancock is recorded by many historians to have ridden his horse slowly down the front lines positions, in the midst of shot and shell, to calm the men. Surely his presence must have impressed the 282 men of the 69th Pa "Irish Volunteers" as they withstood the fire. Yet none mention the incident in letters or recollections.

While the bombardment rained shot and shell into the front line, other men of the 69th who were on detached duty saw and felt the experience. Corporal John Rittenhouse, the regiment's head teamster was with the other nine teamsters of the regiment and five other detached men with the wagon train south on the Taneytown road. At the beginning of the bombardment the regimental and company wagons were moved back southward on the road for protection against the shelling and would remain there until after the battle. Late that afternoon, after the fighting ended, they would be would be brought back up to resupply the men and to allow the cooks and butchers to prepare the first hot meal the lads of the 69 would have since June 30 outside Uniontown. John Flood, John McLane, Sylvester Sossaman and John Prenderville would prepare this long waited meal. Nearby were several others from the 69th who had been attached to Brigade duty: Joseph Crook and William Sullivan from company B would not rejoin the regiment for several days.

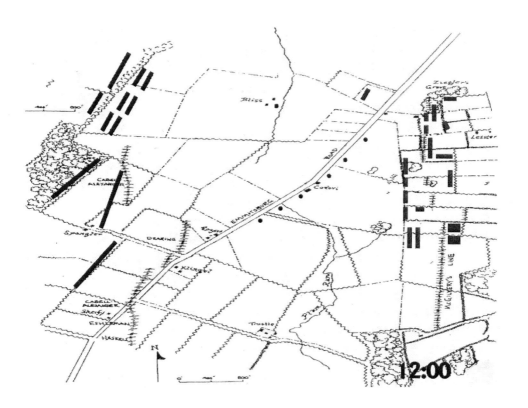

Gettysburg Battlefield July 3, 1863

Regardless of the length of the rebel bombardment, the stage was set and as the men of the 69th looked out over the Valley separating them from the Confederate lines they realized that this battle as going to be very different from the battles they had fought in the past two years. Unlike Glendale and Antietam and Fredericksburg where the 69th Pa "Irish Volunteers" had to charge into the ranks of the enemy, this battle would see the enemy having to charge into the ranks of the 69th. At Glendale the rebels had a hill and trees. At Antietam they were hidden in the woods. At Fredericksburg only last December the Confederates were behind a stone wall on a hill. This time the lads had the stone wall and the hill and this time most were armed with several rifles and had artillery behind them.

Across from the 69th was General George Pickett's Divisioon of Longstreet's Second Corps 5,000 men strong. Beside this division were troops from A.P. Hill's 1st Corps, prepared to follow any breakthrough.

After a few minutes of silence the smoke began to clear and the vast expanse of the Confederate infantry lines became visible. The sight was one that none would ever forget. Private Joseph Garnett, who in company I was highest in elevation and remembered, "The enemy appeared at the edge of the woods and advanced across the field to the Emmittsburg Road and when they were about half way across we opened up on them . . ." Charles Banes, Brigade historian, wrote "The Union batteries increased their fire as rapidly as possible, but this did not for a moment delay the determined advance. The rude gaps torn by the shells and case shot were closed as quickly as they were made. As new batteries opened, the additional fire created no confusion in the ranks of the enemy; it's only apparent effect was to mark the pathway over the mile of advance with the dead and dying. None who saw this magnificent charge of Picket's column, composed of thousands of brave men, could refrain from admiring its grandeur." Anthony McDermott, also in Company I wrote "The Confederate Infantry appears upon the scene emerging from the woods opposite more than ½ mile distant in 2 lines. The first line consisting of Garnett's Brigade with Kemper on his right, Armistead's Brigade being the 2nd line. They were followed by a battery of Artillery, which took on the slope of Seminary Ridge. The appearance of those troops gave a feeling of relief from the dread of being ploughed into shreds or torn into fragments by the solid shot or bursting shell that had so thickly filled the air a few moments before. On came these two charging lines of battle with the precession of troops on parade, and the cool steady marching of veterans, which they were.

As this tidal wave advanced before them, three events occurred simultaneously; a speech, motion to the rear-right and motion to the front.

History records that Colonel Dennis O'Kane loudly spoke to his regiment and urged them to hold their fire and to remember that they were fighting for Pennsylvania and warned against any man shirking his duty. Some veterans of the 69th remember Brigadier General Webb coming down to the front and also speaking to the men. The memories of the lads of the 69th vary . . . to Private Whittick in company E "Our orders were not to fire until we saw the whites of their eyes. I believe that was the order General Webb gave us" . . . McDermott remembers that it was Col. Dennis O'Kane "Our Col. O'Kane ordered the men to reserve their fire until they could plainly distinguish the whites of their eyes. He reminded the command on their being on the soil of their own state and concluding with the words "and let your work this day be for Victory or to the death". He also remembered "We waiting until we could see the whites of their eyes, that was the order as we received it . . ." In the center of the line Hugh McKeever recalled that "General Webb stood up behind our company and said "Boys don't fire until they get over that fence."

Colonel Dennis O'Kane

Perhaps the best summation of the talk that Colonel O'Kane gave to his men would be . . . . *"Men, the enemy is coming, but hold your fire until you see the whites of their eyes. I know that you are as brave as any troops that you will face, but today you are fighting on the soil of your own state, so I expect you to do your duty to the utmost. If any man among you should flinch from that duty, I would ask the man next to him to kill him on the spot." O'Kane reached down with his right arm, unsheathed his sword and raised it above his head. "And let your work this day be for victory or to the death."*

Banes noted "The enemies line of battle left the woods in our front, moved in perfect order across the Emmittsburg road, formed in the hollow in our immediate front several lines of battle under a fire of spherical case shot from Wheeler's and Cushings gun and advanced for the assault." **11** In a letter after the war McDermott noted "Col. O'Kane gave us orders not to fire until the enemy came so close to us that we could distinguish the white of their eyes, he also reminded us that we were upon the soil of our own state and that the enemy would probably make a desperate assault upon us, but we knew we were at least as brave as they were. He did not fear but that we would render an account of ourselves this day that would bring upon us the plaudits of our country and that should any man among us flinch in our duty, he asked that the man nearest him would kill him on the spot. He went along the line speaking encouragement to all the companies. General Web, had also addressed our men on the center and talked in a similar manner and gave them all the encouragement in his power. Their addresses were not necessary as I do not believe there was a soldier in the Regiment that did not feel that he had more courage to meet the enemy at Gettysburg than upon any field of battle in which he had yet been engaged." **12** Hugh McKeever in the center recalled that General Webb told the men "If you do as well today as you did yesterday, I will be satisfied"

As the orders and inspirational speeches were given, the men at the wall wondered just how long their skirmishers would take before returning to position. It seemed to many that they had stayed out too long. Suddenly, the skirmishers began to return to the wall. By staying out on the road, they had slowed the rebel advance and caused the front lines of Garnett's Brigade to form battle lines before they crossed the road. Lieutenant Charles McAnally two days after the battle remembered, "I was in Command of the Skirmishers about one mile to the front & every inch of the ground was well contested until I reached our Regt. The Rebels made the attack in three lines of battle. As soon as I reached our line, I met James (James Hand Co. D). He ran & met me with a Canteen of water. I was near played. He said I was foolish—didn't let them come at once. That the 69th was waiting for them. I threw off my coat and in 2 minutes we were at it" **13** George Hansell who returned to fight with the 69th at the wall remembered "We skirmish there all morning on the third. We staid on the skirmish line until Pickett's men came out after the shelling—they cam up and drove us in. When we were driven in, I came up and fell in with the Sixty-ninth and I fought there some time wit them . . . . I was struck by a piece of shell on the leg (during the shelling) . . . . They got up and started towards us and then their skirmish line got up and of course we had to fall back. We loaded and fired all the way back." **14** Private McDermott recalled that one picket from another regiment had fallen right in front of his company at the wall and that some pickets had been shot **15** Captain James Lynch, in command of the Philadelphia brigade skirmishers reported that "we had lost very heavily. We had lost heavy on the skirmish line" **16** Among these losses were most probably several men from the 69th who were captured and sent south to prison after the battle including Privates Owen Clark, James Elliot and Donohue all who were reported to have been wounded and captured in the Federal and Confederate records. There is also a good chance that Corporal Farrell McGovern of Co A was with the skirmish line and captured there only to be shot while returning from parole July 5th. **17**

The motion to the right and rear of the 69th that probably attracted the attention of many in the 69th during the rebel advance across the fields was the forward movement of the 71st Pa to the wall. As the rebel cannonade slackened General Webb ordered the 71st Pa to move forward and to take up position at the wall to the right of the 69th Pa. Several days after the battle, the commander of the 71st Pa wrote in a letter "Our regiment sought cover behind the crest of the hill during the shelling. At one point three of Cushing's caissons exploded showering companies A & F with wooden splinters. At the conclusion of the bombardment the regiment was brought forward to the front wall / fence position to fire at the advancing rebels under the order of the general. I was then ordered to put the men behind the stone wall but there was not enough room so I ordered Lieutenant Col. Kochersperger to put as many men as he could of the *left wing companies* behind the wall to the right of the cannons brought forth by Cushing to the wall . . . . *The remainder of the regiment* was posted back behind the rear wall in company line under my command." (*Letter from Colonel R. Penn Smith July 17, 1863*) Smith recalled in November of 1867 a similar version of the movement. "Under the order of General Webb, I occupied the position marked "A" joining the 69th on my left, but, on the account of the scarcity of room, I could not operate with ease and satisfaction. The right of my left wing reached to the spot marked "B"—the right wing had either to mass in their rear—extend the line to the right in an open field—and fearfully exposed position—or occupy the one to our right and rear behind a rude stone fence marked "C" (then unoccupied). This last we fortunately did, being comparatively well sheltered—and with having a large pile of loaded guns by our side—they were enabled to keep a constant fire on the advancing enemy" *Letter and map from Colonel R.Penn Smith to Peter Rothermal Nov 25, 1867)* Finally from the reports of the Brigade Historian, we see this account. "The artillery, posted a few paces in the rear on more elevated ground, with infantry supports, were pouring in a ceaseless fire over the heads of the men, who were In hardly less danger from this fire than from that of the enemy. Seeing this, and desirous of saving his men for a final determined resistance, leaving *the left wing*, which was less exposed, in command of Lieutenant Colonel Kochersperger, Colonel Smith posted *the right* behind a rude stone wall to the right and rear of the left wing, which had been entirely unoccupied . . . The *left wing of the regiment*, overcome by vastly superior numbers, was obliged to yield." **18 / 19**

Although ordered to pull out his battery Cushing choose to move the last two guns down to the wall which was now solid with troops of the 69th and the 71st Pa. McDermott noted that as the rebel lines advanced his company was suddenly disrupted by this second forward motion of the last of Cushing two gun's (Number 4 & 5) . . . . "At this time two of Cushing's guns were brought from the crest of the ridge and were placed in position in the ranks of Company I, the right flanking company. "(*McDermott Speech not given*)" "While the enemy was advancing across the space two guns were run down from the crest of the ridge into our company. We had to make space in order to let the guns come to the wall." **20** McDermott wrote later "Cushing had already ordered two pieces from the crest down to the wall, and were placed in our line of battle, with company I, the right flanking company of the regiment and of which I was a private at that time. These pieces done more harm in that position to us than they did the enemy, as they only fired two or three rounds when their ammunition gave out, and one of these rounds blew the heads off two privates of the company, who were on one knee at the time, besides these pieces drew upon us more than our share of fire from the battery which followed Pickett from the woods opposite to us." **21**) The two privates McDermott refers to were Christian Rohlfing who stood 5'7 ½"" tall and Edward Head who stood 5' 8". Both were decapitated by a discharge of Cushings gun number 5. Private Head had joined the 69th at the beginning in August 1861 and had served through the Peninsular campaign. The 22 year old, Head had deserted sometime in the fall of 1862 and was arrested in Philadelphia December 6th and sent first to Fort Delaware and then returned to the regiment. Rohlfing had also joined at the outset at age 21. He was a German Lutheran who supported his widowed mother.

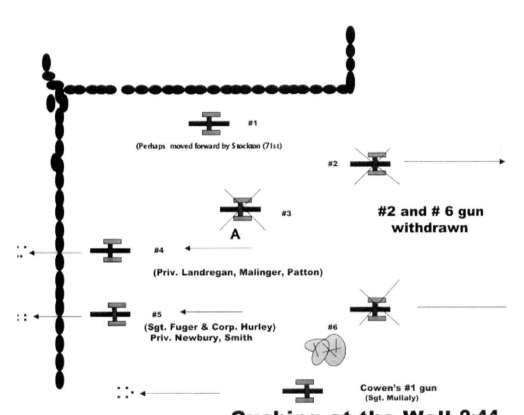

Cushing Shifts Position

This account of the disruption of Company I is supported by the memory of Sergeant Garrett. "I saw two pieces run down by our company to the stone wall" 22. The reasons for placing gun #5 in the midst of Company I of the 69th was because of the topography of the hill. A perfect platform for a gun was located right behind the center of Company I's position. The effect of this would be to fragment Co I of the 69th into two separate sections. Sergeant Garrett remembered the company being "somewhat scattered" 23 (Trial of the 72nd Pa pp. 255). In 1887 McDermott used the phrase "placed in position between the men of Company I—the first company—and commenced firing . . ." 24

It is not clear whether or not the 71st was able to fire a volley at the rebel troops off in the distance, but what is clear is that soon after the entire line advanced there was a need to shift most of the companies backward again. Between the arrival of Gun #5 which stretched Company I of the 69th to the right and the arrival of gun #4 which required more space in the middle of the 71st, the available room was again reduced. Companies C, H, G and K remained at the wall (with about 110 men) with K at the angle. Company B now under the command of Lieutenant Jacob Smallwood had been the company at the angle and had helped run one of Cushing's other guns down toward the angle. However Company B now had to join the right wing of the 71st as they moved backward. The reports of Col. Smith and his hand drawn maps just after the battle suggest the entire right wing retreated to the rear wall and crest position although some accounts suggest that some men of the center companies may have been placed at the connecting wall 25 The largest company of the 71st, remaining at the front wall, with 38 men under 1st Lieutenant Jacob Devine, was Company C just to the right of Company I 69th. Located to their right was gun #4 of Cushing. To the right were smaller companies H, with 29 men, G with 17 men and K with 23 men.

Meanwhile off to the left of companies G and K of the 69th was the 59th New York Regiment which had taken severe casualties both on the 2nd and during the bombardment and was reduced in size at this moment to only119 men. It would be important for the 59th NY to hold its ground to protect the left flank of the 69th Irish Volunteers.

> Out on the skirmish line Captain Stewart of the 72nd observed the forward motion of the rebel forces. "In a conversation with Captain Stewart of the 72nd, who was on the skirmish line and who was lying wounded along the side of the fence that borders the Emmetsburg Road. He said the skirmishers had erected a temporary breastwork of rails and when Pickett's div. Advanced, the house on our left front caused two brigades to pass to the right the other to the left and as

the latter approached the skirmish line, Stewart thinks they must have thought it the main line for they formed line of battle at the time they received the fire of the skirmishers. "Lt McAnally of the 69th was also on the skirmish line. The fence on the Emmetsburg road to our left was mostly destroyed but on our immediate front almost intact. The delay of the single regiment which moved to the left of the house was caused by forming line of battle while the two brigades that moved to the right of the house with no obstruction." Stewart remained where he was wounded the enemy passing over him. After the repulse he came into our lines" **26**

Garnett regiments had now reached the Emmittsburg Road and were crossing. Much of the fence line had already collapsed from the fighting on July 2nd. In fact the First Corps had removed some on July 1 when they moved into position on the first days fight. But some sections remained to slow Garnett's men. All 278 remaining men of the 69th and the 4 companies of the 71st crouched behind the wall ready for combat. There were wounded already to be watched over. The 8 men wounded in the bombardment remained at the wall being cared for by comrades with the exception of Thomas McGrath of Company H who may have been removed to the rear. Many in the 69th checked carefully the extra rifles that lay against the wall and propped against the wood rail and barricade they had constructed. Bodies in Gray from the day before still lay out in the fields—many would soon join them in death. The order had been to wait until the "whites of their eyes were visible but it seems that some men started firing a little early.

As they approached the rail fence, their formation was irregular, and near the front and center were crowded together the regimental colors of the entire Pickett division; the scene strangely illustrated the divine words, "terrible as an army with banners" **27** Most waited for the command before they unleashed a mighty volley. Sergeant Garrett (Co I) on the right recalled, "when they were halfway across we opened up on them and they made a rush up towards the hill and broke in over the wall to our right" **28** In the middle of the line Hugh McKeever "saw them coming along and nobody did any firing, but the men were standing up, but before they got over somebody fired just as they struck the Emmittsburg Road, and our pickets had hardly got in when they came with a rush. They seemed to be coming from our right towards our left, that is they turned as they struck the Emmittsburg road and there were some troops to our left that were firing at them." . . . . About that time somebody said 'stick it to them' or to fire and everyone was loading and firing as fast as they could." **29**

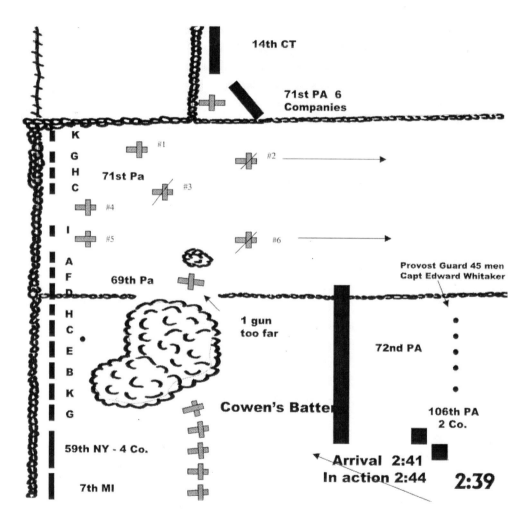

The 69th Company Alignment

"When about two thirds of the field, that lay between the stone wall and Emmittsburg road had been crossed, the enemy changed his direction to an oblique march to his left and kept this direction in a good order, as when marching directly to the front when within 20 yards of us we rec'd the command to fire, our first round was fired with deliberation and simultaneously and threw their line into confusion, from which they quickly rallied and opened their fire upon us." *(McDermott to Bachelder June 2, 1886).* The regiments of Garnett were from North to South the 56th Va. (opposite the 71st Pa); The 28th Va. opposite Companies I, A, F of the 69th; The 19th and 18th Va. and half of the 8th Va., opposite the remainder of the 69th line. In addition a number of men from the 1st Va. of Kemper's line faced the two left companies of the 69th G & K. The combined strength of the men on the 69th line would be about 250 rifles but if we factor in the estimated 400 extra guns of the 69th companies (noting that most of the extra rifles were in possession of the center and left companies) we get a firepower of 650 rifles firing within period of 30 to 45 seconds. This firepower stopped the 19th, 18th & 8th Va. dead in their tracks and probably killed and wounded upwards of 150 of their soldiers. The immediate effect was a halt in Garnett's advance so that the remainder of the rebel troops from these three regiments halted some 30 yards out from the wall. The topography of the field in front of the 69th plays an important role here. There is a swale that runs parallel to the wall out about 30 yards. The dip in the ground at this point is enough to shelter men kneeling down. This is the position that the 19th, 18th and 8th Virginia men took after the terrible effects of the initial volley of the 69th hit them. It is here that they attempted to exchange volleys with the center and left of the 69th line. Until Kemper's and then Armistead's Brigade arrived, it is here that they remained. The view from the rebel lines was one of horror. They must have wondered how one regiment could pour forth such firepower. The Major of the 19th Va. was shot down by a lad of the Sixty ninth who had "a nearly horizontal shot" on him and was hit in the knee and carried back toward the Codori house. **30** Captain Campbell of Co G 18th Va. was one of the first to fall wounded. Captain Henry Owen, who survived, saw men to the right and left of him torn apart by the first volleys of the 69th at the wall. "But all knew the purpose to carry the heights in front and the mingled masses, from fifteen to thirty deep rushed toward the stone wall." **31** In company E of the 18th Va., two brothers faced the rapid volleys of the 69th. Captain Edmund Cocke was grazed by a bullet from the wall and moments later, his brother Lieutenant William Cocke fell dead from another bullet in the murderous fire. **32** The Colonel of the 19th Virginia, Colonel Henry Gantt made it almost to the wall when he was hit by a bullet in the mouth which resulted in "nearly all his teeth neatly and effectively extracted" **33**

Some rebels were hit by multiple bullets Private William Coleman Co A 18th Va. was shot in the left hand, the chest and lost several right fingers to a hail of lead, while his captain and 1st Sergeant took shots in the neck and left arm. Even with slight swale protection, the more than 600 bullets in the first 45 seconds butchered the ranks of the rebels. The fury of the volleys from the 69th tore down most of the flags in the rebel line. Randolph Shotwell in the 8th Virginia watched as "half the flags in Pickett's Division were shot down in the first volley from the wall, "but quickly they were raised by the survivors and borne forward." Shotwell remembered being "stunned, dazed, bewildered" but managed to pick up a musket an fire at the 69th behind the wall **34**

On the right however, things were very different. The 71st Pa began to break apart once they received the first volley from the 56th and 28th Va. In addition the men of companies I, A, F and D probably did not have as many extra rifles and had experienced or witnessed the "friendly fire" of Cushings #5 gun. While the 19th, 18th and 8th Va. stopped short unable to advance in the face of over 650 rifles fired at them in a short span of time, The Virginians of the 56th and 28th did not stop and ran right up to and over the wall. "When the enemy came closeup we were upon our knees, below this wall, watching their movements and just then we poured a volley into the advancing line as they came up. Then the firing became general." wrote Anthony McDermott later.

McDermott noted the earlier actions of the Cushing Battery in his companies midst. "Poor Cushing was struck in the thighs, just previous to the arrival of those two guns on our line. During all that terrible storm of artillery Cushing stood at the wall with our Company, glass in hands watching the effect of each shot from his own guns all of his commands were distinctly heard by our men, he would shout back to his men to elevate or depress their pieces so many degrees, his last command that we heard was 'that's excellent—keep that range' a few moments after as we were rising from the ground to receive the advancing infantry, one of our men called out "that Artillery officers has his legs knocked out from under him". This ended the life of as cool and brave an officer as the Army as possessed of.". **35**

McDermott commented on the Cushing guns during the trial of the 72nd Pa "They opened fire on them and discharged three or four rounds, perhaps more, when their fire ceased and the cannoneers disappeared leaving their guns with us." . . . And "The gunners left us leaving their guns behind, hence they were useless" **36** "The troops on our right abandoned their position which left a blank space . . ." **37** The trial mentioned above occurred many years after the war when the 72nd Pa sued in court to have their monument placed along the wall occupied by the 69th and 4 companies of the 71st.

The perspective of the attacking Virginia troops was one of opportunity. Lieutenant George Finley (56th Va. Co K) remembered that the charge up the last part of the hill was done in silence, only the occasional complaint from the men that they were not permitted to fire. Then within about 75 yards out the first of the 71st Pa men began to break and a volley was ordered and then another. The first line reached the stone wall and were greeted with shouts of "Don't shoot! We surrender! "Where shall we go?' The captives from Companies G, H & C of the 71st Pa were pulled across the wall and told to go unescorted back toward the Emmittsburg Road." **38**

Not all the men of the 71st Pa ran or were captured. In Company K at the angle Sergeant Thomas Cosgrove and Corporals John Dugan and James Haggerty were killed at the wall as were Privates Ruben Miller and Levi Dellinger. Sergeant Andrew Monahan and Corporal Quinn were both wounded and fell to the ground with Private George Fitzgibbons. A group of 5 men from Company K would be taken prisoners and held at the wall during the fighting, to be rescued later. Company C, the largest of the four companies with 38 men, next to the 69th company I had one killed (Private Robert Wallin) and 4 wounded but lost their commander 1st Lieutenant Jacob Devine as prisoner along with Corporal Hill and two privates. In the middle, Company G had all four of their Sergeants wounded trying to rally their men and Private Matthew Smith fell dead at the wall. Two more would be taken captive (Corp Gallagher and Private Nelson) also in the center, Company H had four killed in position including Sergeant Franz Vonderfer and three taken captive. They also suffered 6 men wounded in the fight. Altogether 10 men from the 71st would be taken as prisoners and sent south. **39**

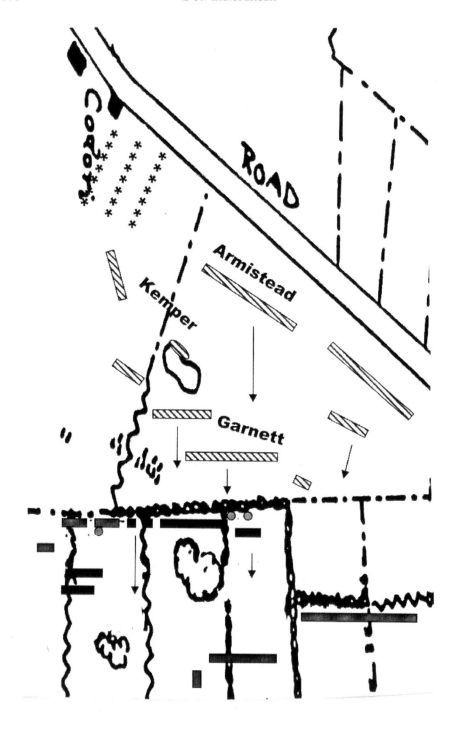

The Advance of Pickett's Division

Sensing a void was about to appear to their right, either Colonel O'Kane or Lieutenant Colonel Tschudy shouted to their right companies to "refuse the right" . . . to swing toward the trees.

Rebel Lieutenant Finley was elated when he saw men from the Tennessee regiment of Frye's Brigade also arrived at the wall and cross over. Suddenly rebels from Virginia and Tennessee were jumping over the wall. Finley looked back to see General Garnett still on his horse just to his rear. Then a volley from the crest marked the arrival of the 72nd Pa. The volley killed Garnett and caused the few Confederates who had jumped the wall to return. For 30 seconds (while Armistead's brigade was closing on the wall) volleys were exchanged between the 72nd Pa outlined on the top of the crest in the horizon light and the 56th and 28th Virginia, protected by the stone wall. The 72nd Pa clearly got the worst of the exchange with over 50 men killed or wounded in 30 seconds. Then the 72nd Pa "fell back behind the crest, leaving us still in possession of the stone wall" **40** From the perspective of the 72nd Pa Private Thomas Reed in Company F remembered, "As we got to the top of the hill we got there just in time that the rebels reached the stone wall and we engage them immediately when we got there. The musketry continued I should say, twenty minutes—twenty or twenty five minutes." **41**

Major Samuel Roberts of the 72nd reported on the firing from the crest "when the right company was dressed back upon the regiment to the left and the regiment had come to a front, we took the fire of the enemy and at that time I judged that not less than eighty of our men fell, firing commenced then at will, and what men had advanced over the stonewall fell back: I mean the enemy, and used that stone wall, the same as a barricade, the enemy could neither advance or retreat, and abut the center of that wall they (the enemy) placed their colors. All our color bearers except one had been disabled as we were in that line formed there some sixty yards from the west wall." **42** Lieutenant Frederick Boland (Co B 72nd Pa) and his Captain were both wounded at the top of the crest after the rebels crossed the wall "I was hit by one of the first volleys of the enemy. Then I got away as quick as possible. I thought it was no place for me . . . . to the right of the clump of trees." **43**

The losses of the 72nd at the crest were noted by Charles Banes after the battle, "The principle portion of the men laid on the crest at the position they had occupied. Probably from ten to twenty feet in front of it. It was remarkable how many men were lying in a line. If they had been laid there by their comrades they could not have been laid more in a line." **44**

It is all together probable that the panic that swept the 4 companies of the 71st Pa also soon swept the men of the right side of Company I 69th PVI. Sergeant Joseph Garrett who was in the center of Company I reports "they made a rush up the hill and broke in over the wall to our right. We were ordered to fall back and face the parties crossing the wall. (We were) at right angles to the wall after we halted. I was opposite the clump of trees when I stopped" Garrett remembered swinging back and did not see Private McDermott with him.**45**

Anthony McDermott records his personal actions thusly "We fell back, not in good order but in some order, towards the crest of the hill and kept up the fire upon Armistead and his fellows.**46**

And elsewhere he remembered "Co I & A quickly changed and moved back to the crest to get between Armistead and Cushings four pieces"**47** The advance companies of the Seventy-first are literally crowded out of place by the enemy and with one company of the Sixty-ninth, they form with the remainder of Colonel Smith's command at the stone fence. **48** McDermott confirms this account, "After getting near the crest, we got a little in advance of Armistead and then we stood and fired upon him and his men. We maintained the fire along with a cross fire delivered by the men of the 71st, in the Angle until Armistead had fallen wounded."**49**

It is clear then that some of company I retreated directly eastward to the crest while others shifted in a "refusal of the right" motion to join companies A and D. When McDermott reached the crest he remembered, "I was afraid we were going to get whipped and as I had done in every other fight, which was to study our rear and to know what support we might rely on when pushed. I saw the 72nd Penn in line in their original position Adj. Genl. of the brigade Captain H. Banes was on horse riding along the line of the 72nd urging the men to come up to our aid, while at the same time Genl. Webb stood on the crest facing the 72nd, and of course his back to the stone wall." **50** Joining McDermott at the crest were most probably the other men of the right wing of the company, which would include 1st Sergeant William Richardson, Corporal Henry Souder and Privates William White, George Diechler and William Frazier. Quite possibly Private John Ellison, who was wounded in the leg, began racing up the hill with them. McDermott's tent mate Thomas Diver, who had become close with his family, was already dead at the front wall from a head shot during the cannonade. It is possible that Private John

Boyle also was killed at the wall early. Private George Diechler was wounded in the groin at some point in the fighting. Corporal Souder received a fatal round in the lungs sometime during the fight.

Private George Diechler—Company I

McDermott's account which suggests that Armistead came over the wall at the same time as the shift of Companies I & A and the capture of company F, ignores the fact that there was a distance between the Garnett line and the Armistead line of at least 50 yards and that action took place at the wall BEFORE Armistead arrived. When McDermott and those of the right flank of Company I retreated directly backward, they were in motion at the same time the 56th Va. reached and came over the wall. McDermott and his comrades must have reached the crest beside the 71st just before the volley of the 72nd took place. By the time they were again engaged, Company F had already been captured and only then Armistead reached the wall. McDermott admits not seeing company F taken captive in his testimony at the 72nd Pa Monument trial. **51**

The ten captives from the 71st Pa now hurried back toward the approaching regiments of Armistead's brigade. Artillery fire from Cowen's battery now in place to the rear and left of the 69th's left flank made their journey to captivity perilous. 1st Lieutenant Jacob Devine and Corporals Jesse Hill from Company C plus Corporal Andrew Gallagher from Company G hurried the 7 privates (Woods, Nelson, Bradley, Hafferty, Kelly, Kensalla and Perkins) . . . most would die in rebel prisons. Armistead's regiments were over the fences but still far from the wall. **52**

At the wall with Company A, John Harvey Sr. prepared to leave his wounded and semi-conscious son against the wall before he and his first Sergeant Ralph Rickby and Corporal Patrick Moran could join in the refusal to the right. The wall provided some protection but after his father left him, John Harvey Jr. would receive a bullet wound in the left arm and probably be trampled upon by rebels who were soon to leap the wall. At some point in the fighting 1st Sergeant Rickby was hit in the left side of his neck by a bullet and felt the sting all down his left arm. The damage to his left arm nerves would remain the rest of his life. Before Company A withdrew, they had already taken some losses from the volleys of the 56th and 28th Virginia regiments. The tall and lanky Sergeant Edward Bushell may have tripped or stayed too long at the wall. He was captured to be sent back to Seminary Ridge and then south. He would imprisoned, paroled and then die of disease in 1864 from his ordeal. Private Patrick O'Brien was killed instantly by a bullet in the head. Private Robert Morrison was killed by a bullet in the chest. Private John Dunn was hit in the right elbow. Private Frederick Bevensted took two bullets, one in the lung and one in the abdomen and died during the fighting.

As the men of Company I on the left side with Sergeant Garrett joined with Company A in their rush past the Company F position, the men of Co F still stood and kneeled firing at the enemy. Their Captain, George Thompson had been hit in the mouth with a bullet and they were about to be engulfed by the 28th Virginia. "Co F seemed to either not have received the order in time or had no desire to leave the wall, hence an opening was left behind which left the enemy get between them and our two flanking Companies. They rushed in on the rear of our main line and it looked as though our Regiment would be annihilated, the contest here became a hand to hand affair, Company F was completely hustled over the stone wall into the enemy's ranks and were all captured, their Captain Thompson being killed and their two Lieutenants wounded and prisoners." **53** Hugh McKeever is the center of the regiment was told about the fate of Company F by his comrades "I was told then and there that it had a gap. That was the reason Company F was captured. When the rebels came over the company was captured entirely because Thompson, the captain, was killed before he could give the order . . . . After the fight was over, I had in Company F a cousin that had been killed and he had been like a father to me. I was quite young at the time and I heard he was killed when—" **54**

Although many men in the 69th believed that Company F had been swallowed whole by the rebel attack (consequently many historians since have expressed this view), in fact many of the company members were able to join in the "right refusal". When Captain Thompson was hit in the mouth and killed instantly no command was issued but the men on the rear rank soon saw Company A moving by. The taller men on the right flank of the company had the farthest to move and were frequently captured. The tallest man in the company, Patrick Harvey at 6' 1 ½" was able to escape and fight on hand to hand with Company D (he would desert 3 days after the battle) but Corporal Henry Thomas standing in front of Harvey would take a bullet in the leg and fall to the ground and later die in Baltimore of lockjaw tetanus. Behind the right side of the line 1st Sergeant Robert Doak was captured. The next two in the front line Peter Smith at 5'7" and Arthur Mulholland at 5'7 ½" would be taken and sent over the wall to southern prison camps where they would both die. Just behind them at the right end of the line Privates George Gilpin, James Hand and John Fullerton all tall men would escape toward the trees. In the center of the company Corporal Davis Haggerty was struck in the skull with a minie ball that smashed in his upper cheek and left him on the ground and scarred for life. Around him Private Joseph Dunbar was hit in the left forearm but was able to flee. Private John McKinney was captured and would later died in Richmond. However, rear rank privates Condon, Gallagher Laycock and Clark all avoided capture. The greatest numbers of prisoners taken from Company F were among officers and non-comms. Sgts George Mulholland and John O'Neill were both captured while Sgts John

Gregg and Thomas Kerr escaped. Both of the Lieutenants of the company 1st Lieutenant John Ryan and 2nd Lieut. John Eagan were captured. Shorter men in the front line and the left end of the line were frequent causalities. Private Thomas Lindsay was hit in the left thigh while kneeling and loading on his knee and left on the ground. The bullet that struck him would pass into his hip joint. Private John Dolan who had been hit with a shell fragment earlier avoided capture. Patrick Leister, Patrick Rafferty and Arthur McLaughlin all privates were taken prisoner and hustled over the wall into captivity. On the left wing of the company Private Michael Gorman was seized., Private Neil McCaffery was killed in hand to hand fighting and Privates Fleming and Henry Allen (the shortest man in the unit at 5'4") both were wounded but escaped captured. Fleming probably fell to the ground with a serious wound. The toll in Company of the 25 men on the firing line would be one killed instantly, 7 captured and 4 wounded too badly to move. This would allow 13 to escape. Two of these men Privates Thomas Lafferty and Hugh Lynch received leg wounds sometime during the fighting that did not require amputations. Among the 8 officers and Sgts behind the line, Captain Thompson was killed, 5 were captured and only two escaped.55 / 56

First Lieutenant John Ryan—Company F

The collapse and capture of the men of Company F was remembered from the Confederate perspective of Sergeant Drewry Easley of the 14th Virginia. As Armistead approached the wall Easley rushed forward to the left of his regiment and ran directly into a group of Yankee prisoners with their hands up in the air who were heading down the hill toward the road. His first reaction was to bring down his bayonet but realized that they were out of the fight and pushed through them to reach the wall. 57

Major John Corbett Timberlake later wrote that the brigade "had nearly reached the stone fence, when there was a rush of prisoners through our lines that I exclaimed, 'the day is ours'"

Further down the hill two rebels from the 18th Virginia Captain Campbell and Private Clay (Co G) had been wounded by the massive volley from the 69th line and had sought protection at the rock outcropping known as the knoll. As they lay there, their regiment along with the 19th and part of the 8th Virginia continued to trade fire with the 69th Pa. Armistead's brigade passed by and then, all of a sudden, two Union soldiers who had surrendered passed by and the four men all worked their way toward the Emmittsburg Road. During this movement back to Seminary ridge the Union soldiers told them of the death of General Garnett. 58

The most critical moment of the battle was now at hand because the "right refusal" was uneven and incomplete. Company F had been largely eliminated. More than one hundred rebels had leaped the wall and were entering the bushes and trees and coming behind the 69th line. Some men from Companies I and A and F never got the chance to take their stand. They were killed or wounded before the line formed at the trees. From Company I 2nd Lieutenant Edward Harmon would be hit in the left hand, the bullet passing through the back side and tearing the muscles to the middle fingers. Sergeant Patrick McMahon would be hit with a minie ball in the right thigh. John Dolan of Company F would receive a bullet in his right thigh, which would drop him on the field. Private Robert Crooks from Company A was hit in the right side of his neck by a bullet that passed through and exited below the jaw on the opposite side.

What made survival possible is that in order to buy time for the remaining men of Companies I, A & F to get in order and begin fighting, a group from Company D was ordered by Captain Tinen to countercharge the Virginians

Captain Patrick Tinen—Company D (postwar)

rushing toward the gap between the back of Company D and the disorganized "right refusal' troops. Lieutenant McAnally of Company D was in the middle of it . . . "I threw off my coat and in 2 minutes we were at it—hand to hand they charged on us twice and we reputed them. They tried the Regiment on our Right and drove them which caused us to swing back our right then we charged them on their left flank & in the charge James fell (Private James Hand Co D). May the Lord have mercy on his soul? He never flinched from his post and was loved by all that knew him . . . . He received a ball through the breast & one through the heart and never spoke after." **59**

As rebels broke through into the trees the right and center of the 69th was being attacked from three sides. "Many of the enemy were here mingled with our own men some so close that while they struck at each other with the barrels of their rifles, they could not inflict any disabling injury." **60** "The adjoining company, D, having more time, were enable to turn upon and hold the enemy at bay, using their muskets as clubs, the enemy doing likewise" **61**

Along with Charles McAnally and James Hand in that quick countercharge charge was their good friend Sergeant James McCabe. "This letter will answer for Sergt. McCabe. He was shot through the head. He died in 2 minutes after." Also in the charge was Sergeant Jeremiah Gallagher who was, according to McAnally, "riddled with bullets" **62** In the hand to hand fighting on their front and on their right, Company D took terrible loses. Lieutenant McAnally was cut with a saber on the head; Corporal Patrick Carney and Corp James McCann were both mortally wounded. Carney would linger in a Harrisburg hospital until July 29th when he would die of blood poisoning. McCann would die shortly after the fighting ended. Private William Hayes was hit in the head with a bullet, as was Private John Williams. The wounded included Corporal Patrick Connelly (with a bullet in his left hip) and Private John Donovan. "We stood and faced them, when a hand to hand conflict took place. Men went down all around me that day, many of them to rise no more", remembered Lieutenant Michael Fay. "By this time they had got so close that men were fighting each other hand to hand. We were at too close quarters to fire, so at the last we battered the "rebs" on the head with our guns" said Sergeant David Kiniary. **63** Bullets through the right thigh and the right calf ended the service career of Private Thomas Clark who would be discharged only after a year in the hospital. Private John Nester would take a bullet in his left leg and would later in the war take another in the same leg at the Battle of Wilderness. Private Charles McErland, who had already suffered shell shock during the bombardment, was also hit in the right knee with a bullet.

The combat was fierce and bloody "Kemper's men, some of whom I believe used their musket butts as clubs as well as some of our men, as an instance, Corporal Bradley of Co. D who was a quite savage sort of fellow, wielded his piece, striking right and left, and was killed in the melee by having his skull crushed by a musket in the hands of a rebel, and Private Donnelly of the same company, used his piece as a club, and when called upon to surrender replied tauntingly, 'I surrender' at the same time striking his would be captor to the ground. I cite these two instances because they seem to have been particularly noticed by their comrades and spoken of by many of the men of the above mentioned Co." . . . . "Many of the men of the above mentioned company had been spoken of being struck, but not sufficiently to send them to the hospital" **64** "In his testimony at the 72nd Pa trial Anthony McDermott described the actions of Company D this way "Company D were better prepared and they turned and fought them hand to hand, and one man that I saw had his skull crushed with a musket ad that night I hard that another one had been struck by one of the enemy with the barrel of his piece when he called to him, to surrender" **65**

Before the fighting ended there would be a total of 9 killed and 14 wounded from Company D of the 69th. Killed would include Private Charles Jenkins who was shot in the stomach and Private Patrick Coniff was wounded. From Co I, which had refused the line, Private Michael Logan was found dead near the trees after the battle. He had been killed instantly by a bullet in the chest. Private William Elben from the same company was hit in the right knee with a minie ball in the fight. In the midst of the reformed right line, Lieutenant Colonel Martin Tschudy, already with a wounded head from the day before took a bullet in the bladder while rallying his men and died shortly thereafter. Near him acting Sergeant Major Thomas Norman was wounded as well.

> At the height of the fighting, General Webb ran back to the Flag Sergeant of the 72nd Pa who stood with his regiment at the crest of the hill firing at the rebels downhill at the wall. Webb wanted the 72nd to advance on the wall. Color Sergeant William Finecy held the flag firm as Webb ordered him and the rest of the regiment to advance down the slope. Finecy would not budge and refused to move. For a moment a tug of war ensued between the two men, Sergeant Finecy ignoring the Brigadier Generals uniform and stripes. The color company refused to budge and Webb recalled later returning downhill to the flank of the 69th Pa where the hand to hand fighting continued. Color Sergeant Finecy would be pierced with several bullets within seconds of this incident. Whether this occurred before the 72nd pulled back from the crest or as it was advancing back to the crest is unclear. **66**

At this point, McDermott seems to have left the cluster of the 71st and 1st Sergeant Richardson, Corporal Souder and Privates White, Frazer and Diechler of his own company and ran over toward the copse of trees toward General Webb. "I ran to General Webb who had his back to us, and touched him on the shoulder and told him that their leader had fallen and that the enemy were running away. As I touched General Webb on the shoulder, he looked around and saw Armistead lying almost in front of one of Cushing's guns (Gun # 3) on the crest of the hill. General Webb repeated almost my words and urged the line behind the crest (the 72nd Pa) to "come up, boys, the enemy is running" 67

In Harrow's First brigade reserve, private Alfred Carpenter in the 1st Minnesota watched to his right the behavior of the 72nd Pa at the crest of the hill,

> "On our immediate right a three years' Philadelphia regiment, the 72nd Pennsylvania, was ordered to charge. They advanced a short distance wavered, fell back, and could not be got forward. On our immediate left a regiment of nine month's men from Vermont Green Mountain boys, numbering between three and four hundred men more than our whole brigade, when ordered to charge, advanced across the field into that fire with as much apparent coolness, as much steadiness and with as perfect a line as I ever saw a regiment of veterans pass in review on a gala day. Vermont stock suddenly rose, while Pennsylvania went down below zero." 68

> From the same position, Major Harry Abbott of the 20th Massachusetts later described his observations of the 72nd Pa's behavior, "Baxter's Pennsylvania men had most disgracefully broken and the rebels were within our line." 69 / 70

> Captain James Lynch of the 106th Pa later moved down to the wall as the fighting ended and surveyed the scene "The Seventy-First had evidently been run over and the right of the Sixty-ninth. I saw one of the men of the Sixth-ninth lying across the wall with head hanging on our side and his body over the rebel side" 71

During the first wave assault by Garnett's Brigade, the left of the 69th, companies G and K and B acted in unison with the center companies E, C, H, D by firing devastating volleys at the 19th, 18th and 8th Virginia. With several guns to a man their first three to five volleys occurred within moments. However, just before the arrival of Armistead's Brigade, the left of the regiment encountered two new developments that would effect their ability to hold their position. First, men from Kemper's Brigade occupied the slash of rocks directly in front of the 59th New York and the 7th Michigan and began firing from this protected area into the flank of companies G & K. Secondly there is reason to believe that much of the 59th New York (four companies were on the line with about 119 men at this time) bolted for the rear. 72

This left a space that was quickly occupied by rebels from the left of Kemper's brigade. Kemper's Brigade was being hit hard by the Vermont Yankees who were firing into the rebel right flank. This resulted in even more fire into the left of the 69th Pa. This arrival of Kemper's men is what Whittick and McKeever referred to as the second of the three assaults. The third assault (The arrival of Armistead's 9th and 14th Virginia) would push the left of the 69th to the limit. As John Buckley who was a private in Company K saw it "I remember when Pickett's men advanced up to the wall. Our company swung around in a half circle to the umbrella trees. The umbrella trees were larger more extended. They covered more space than they do at the present time (1890). Our men fought back all the way to their position at the wall. I know the rebels crossed over the right and crossed over me." 73 In some places the Confederates from Armistead's right regiments not only reached the wall but also jumped over it. 5 foot 10 inches tall, Private Michael McCormack (Co K), who had recurrent leg injuries from Fredericksburg had been wounded in the left shoulder and in the right leg by this time and lay right at the wall. As he lay at the wall several rebels walked on him or jumped down from the wall on him smashing his right leg. He ended up with a hernia and ruptures from having been trampled under foot at the wall. McDermott in his short history of the 69th written in 1887 states "Some of the men in their desperation actually passed over the wall, through the lines of the Sixty-ninth, on its left, but never to return, as they sank to the ground in death, pierced with bullets . . ."74. This hand to hand, face to face combat was remembered by the rebels as well. Corporal Jesse Young of the 7th Virginia was hit in the face with a bullet as he carried the regimental flag to the wall. He fell and the flag fell beside him. Suddenly an officer of the 69th stood up and pointed a revolver at him and fired. Young threw up his hands and the bullet found its mark in his right elbow. 75 Beside Young, Private Tolbert grabbed the flag and stepped to the wall. He was shot in the face and fell across the all in front of the 69th. 76 One of his comrades remembered a Union soldier reaching out to grab the flag as Tolbert fell. 77

It is important to remember that the massive volleys that the 69th was able to deliver against Garnett's regiments were linked to each man having several rifles for their use. By the time the second and then third assault occurred, both sides were firing in a more typical one rifle per man pattern and the low wall in front of the 69th offered some but not complete protection. It is in the third assault where most of the killed and wounded occurred including

Colonel Dennis O'Kane, who took a bullet in the abdomen from which he died the next day. As the battle ended, he would be carried down to the care of Surgeon Burmeister at the Frey barn and then transferred to the Second Corps Hospital but died the next morning. The bullet which hit Major James Duffy in the right thigh occurred during the "third" assault. The wound to Major Duffy, who was positioned behind the left flank of the regiment back toward the trees, had profound physical and political effects. From all accounts the bullet that hit him in the right thigh shattered into pieces that lodged in various areas of his upper leg. As soon as the attack ended, his personal servant, Private George H Haws detailed from Company A, would care for him. After quick treatment at the regiment aid station, somehow Haws arranged transportation for Major Duffy all the way through Baltimore to Philadelphia and arrived there July 5 so that the Major could get care from family physicians. Haws disappeared after reaching Philadelphia and was never seen again by the men of the 69th. Rumors were that he joined the navy or the merchant marine. Meanwhile, the wound to Major Duffy was severe. The painful recovery would take several months and even when he would return to the regiment complications would set in and result in a discharge from the service. Duffy tried to return to service but found his chances blocked and became involved in a political battle that would last for months into 1864.

The men who faced the rebels with Companies D and A and parts of F and I write only of two assaults because the Kemper regiments did not stretch as far north as their location. On the left, the five guns of Andrew Cowen's battery were firing canister directly at Kemper's men in the slash and at the knoll. When Armistead's big push comes up at the 69th left flank, Cowen's gunners fired canister shot at the rebel masses. Buckley wrote, "there was a battery there firing, directly in rear of the left companies of the Sixty-ninth regiment. I didn't know what battery it was at the time. They were firing grape and canister over, and it killed some of our men. It sometimes threw up stones. I was hit by a stone and got a lump from it. I found out later that it was Cowen's battery. The battery disappeared as quick as it came. It didn't stay there until the end of the firing." **78** The two men mentioned by Buckley were from company G. They were Privates Clay and Coyle, two friends who had shifted from the 27th Pa to the 69th. They were the two tallest men in the company at 6 foot and 5'9" and each was hit in the back of the head by a cannon blast.

The Laracy brothers (Michael & James) may also have been victims of Cowen "friendly fire" as they both had head and shoulder wounds. But the 8 killed and 11 wounded of Company G at the end of the 69th left wing were also due to rebel fire. Sergeant John O'Conner took a bullet in the head and was killed instantly. Five foot ten inch Private Richard McErland was shot in the head. To his right, Corporal Cyrus O'Daniel was hit twice, hit first by a bullet through his right shoulder and then by a piece of fragment in his right side probably from the same round that Cowen's guns fired into James Clay, who stood beside him. The end of the line was an area of violence and pain. 2nd Lieutenant Michael Mullen had his left hip fractured by a gunshot and would die July 7th. Sergeant Hugh Kelly took several bullets and lingered on in the 2nd Corps hospital until July 20th. Sergeant John Wogan died from a bullet in the stomach. Privates James Rice and James McIntyre were killed instantly at their positions. First Lieutenant Bernard Sherry recalled how Private Hugh Blakely spin around as a bullet hit him in the left shoulder. There were gruesome wounds for others as rebels fired from the protection of the knoll and the slash and from the wall once held by the 59th New York. Private Patrick Colgan had a bullet fracture his left ribs and enter his chest and also was hit in the mouth by a minie ball. He would spend ten months in a hospital before being discharged from the service. Private Patrick Murphy was hit by bullets both in his left shoulder and through his right hand. He would recover only after 6 months. Private William Smiley took a bullet in his left thigh and lived but Private James Scinnader took a bullet to the chest and was reported to have died later. His tragic death was made more so by the loss of his body at the hospital. We know that his wife and family never saw him again and that his 1st Lieutenant Bernard Sherry reported "He lay on the field until the action was over and I ordered him to be carried to the field Hospital after which he was not heard from." Today he lies in a grave marked "Unknown". Finally, Private Cornelius Coakley took a bullet in his right leg, recovered only to take another in his right thigh at the Wilderness. The toll on Company G would include 3 of the five Sergeants. and all of the Corporals.

Col. Arthur Devereux commanding the 19th Mass infantry to the south summed up what happened to the 69th left wing this way. "The Sixty ninth was on the right of Hall's Brigade. There was a little country road here. Their left was directly in front of the copse of trees and they extended out to the right as far as they went, but what distance it was I could not say. I have always insisted upon it that that regiment stood there until it was run over. They would not move. They could not resist the force of the enemy and it appeared to me that they stood there until they were entirely enveloped" **79**

Deveraux's Adjutant William Hill watched the action at the left of the 69th Pa, "The regiment that I knew was the Sixty-ninth Pennsylvania, and it was down by the stone wall all the time, even after the enemy came in the rear of them . . . . The sixty-ninth appeared to be fighting on their own hook. They did not yield one inch and the enemy swarmed right over them but whenever they got a chance to get in a shot here and there they would let the enemy have it. They seemed to be, saying, from the edge of the copse of trees to the middle of it. They found that they were surrounded by troops on three sides, the front the flank and the rear, and the men were fighting them wherever they found them, regardless of any orders or formation . . . the colors were there and where the colors are the regiment is supposed to be: the men were rallying under these colors." **80**

Buckley's own company (K) suffered 2 killed and 4 wounded in the July 3 attack. "His company was (normally) the left flanking one of the regiment but at the battle of Gettysburg Co G was on the left owing to their being left behind somewhere, before we reached the battlefield . . . the men on the left of the Regiment were crouched down behind the wall on one or both knees and that some of Pickett's men actually stepped over them." **81** 2nd Lieutenant John Johnson was shot through the back of the head and assumed dead by many in his regiment. He recovered and was discharged in December. Sergeants Crout and Bradley were both wounded as well. Crout deserted shortly after Gettysburg and Bradley, who had a gunshot wound in his left hip, entered the Reserve Invalid Corps but deserted shortly thereafter. Surprisingly all 6 corporals made it through the fight without a scratch. Private James Kelly was hit in the head with a bullet and died instantly, standing beside Corporal Whitecar. Private Francis Gleeson took a bullet in his shoulder and died August 2 after amputation in Philadelphia. Gettysburg would be his first and last fight. William McNichols who suffered a head wound on July 2, chose to stay on the line and survived the third days fight. Private Bernard Diamond was also wounded at the wall with a bullet that entered his right breast and came out his right shoulder. The rebels pressed right up to the wall and Buckley recalls that he and others in Company K actually pulled back a few yards from the wall at times to avoid being grabbed and pulled over by the Confederates. **82** ". . . . almost every man had from two to five guns that were loaded and were not used until Pickett got within fifty yards of the wall, the slaughter was terrible, to which fact—the ground was literally covered with the enemy's dead bore ample testimony. A great many incidents happened which I could give you but I often think of the men that charged us and I would rather not relate the, as for myself I was in the one position during both charges and only moved a few feet—when Pickett's braves reached the wall." **83** Buckley remembered practically being captured by rebels in the 53rd Virginia regiment who had their hands on him and were pulling at his coat. **84**

Corporal James Whitecar—Company K

Company B next toward the center had been badly mauled on July 2 and suffered three wounded (Sergeant John Britt with an arm wound, Private George Campbell with bullet wound in his left ankle and Private James Merrylees wounded in the left tibia with a bullet).

The only surviving Field officer, Major Peyton of the 19th Virginia, on the Confederate side of this fighting later said, "His strongest and last line was instantly gained; the Confederate battle flag waved over his defenses and the fighting over the wall became hand to hand, and of the most desperate character; but more than half having already fallen, our line was found too weak to rout the enemy. We hoped for support on the left but hoped in vain. Yet a small remnant remained in desperate struggle" **85**

With regard to individual casualties from the center and the left wing, it is hard to know with certainty if these men were hit during the exchange with Garnett's regiments or when the final push came that reached the wall.

   The perspective from the center of the 69th line with both flanks pressured backwards was seen by Private Robert Whittick in the color guard. "As the enemy advanced, the first line, we gave it to them . . . . Finally, the first line wavered, and then the second line came up, and when the third line came up, (Authors note: "first line" was Garnett's right regiments (19th-18th-8th Va., "second line" was Kemper's left regiments (3rd & 7th Va.); "third line" was Armistead's right regiments (53rd & 9th & 14th Va.) that was the time there was a breakup on the right of us, and then the enemy came in our rear, and came down by those bushes we cut down, a lot of trees in our rear were cut down, and they got into us there. That is the time our men commenced clubbing one another. Our colors retreated back about six or eight feet probably, maybe, a little farther. We could not go beyond those woods, because it was all cut down and there was more danger tramping over the trees in the position we had there than if we stood still. Then as near as I can judge, all hands were together." **86** The National colors were held by Sergeant Michael Brady and the Regimental green flag was probably held by Sergeant Davis Kiniary. The cut trees and scrubs of the copse made walking difficult and any backward motion would result in a likelihood of soldiers tripping over stumps and fallen logs.

   From the Confederate perspective, the final push to the wall came when Armistead's regiments piled up behind the remnants of Garnett's force. Captain Owen of the 18th Va., recalled the sound of Armistead arriving "that heavy thud of a muffled tread of armed men . . . the roar and rush of tramping feet of Armistead's column from the rear . . . now the push was on again to the wall" What was left of Garnett's troops leaped to their feet and charged forward mixed with Armistead's 53rd, 9th and 3rd regiments. Some reached the wall and hand to hand combat began. One rebel from the 18th Virginia, who returned with the third assault, described the fight this way, Men fire into each other's faces not five feet apart. There were bayonet thrusts, sabre strokes, pistol shots, cool deliberate movements on the part of some; hot passionate, desperate efforts on the part of others; recklessness of life, tenacity of purpose, fiery determination, oaths, yells, curses, hurrahs, shoutings" **87**

The rebels began pouring in from every side. In questioning during the Trial of the 72nd Pa, Hugh McKeever, who was in the center of the regiment made it clear how nearly surrounded the 69th was.

Q—"The enemy poured in through that gap?
A—Yes, sir to the right of the other two companies and to the left.
Q—And the enemy poured in between the companies of your regiment?
A—Yes, Sir
Q—Was there a considerable number of rebels coming in through there?
A—yes sir they were pretty thick" **88**

In the center of the 69th Pa were companies E, C & H. these companies were able to keep up a constant rate of fire from the time the Garnett regiments appeared until the Armistead line pushed to the wall itself. Sergeant Patrick Taggart of Company E was shot through his right wrist as the ball entered from the side but continued to lead on his men to keep the rebels at bay. As they huddled against the wall, several others received arm wounds. Private Anthony Barnes was hit in the right forearm and shortly afterward by a pistol ball fired from a Confederate officer into his right thigh. Private Hugh McAfee was hit in the left arm and Private Hugh Dornan, who had been wounded during the bombardment in the right leg, was grazed by a bullet in his right elbow. Corporal Cummings, still senseless from the concussion, remained at the walls the pressure mounted on both flanks; the pressure from the rebels to the center front seems to have lessened for a short time. Company C was the flag company and stood in the center of the regiment and had only one death on July 3. 1st Sergeant William Coogan was hit by a bullet in the hip and died July 21 at Second Corps hospital. Corporal Thomas Fagan would take Coogan's place to rally the line and be rewarded with the First Sergeant position after the battle. The several men wounded included Private James Duff who was hit with two bullets one in the back and the other in his left side and Private Michael Toner who was struck by a bullet on his right elbow resulting in a one-year stay in the hospital. A bullet grazed Private John Smith on the right arm. Private John Ward would be unwounded that day but the trauma of the hand to hand fight would result in the Donagal born 38 year old transfer to the regimental hospital corps for the remainder of the war. For Corporal William Farrell, this would be his last day with the 69th. He would be slightly wounded and would shortly desert only to join the US Marines in the fall of 1863 until a fake name (William Giblin) and serve for the remainder of his life as a career soldier. His disagreements with his officers would dictate his future. Just in front of Corporal Farrell, the Lieutenant Col. of the 18th Virginia, Henry Carrington, would fall carrying the regimental flag right up to the wall **89**

Company H, which was the smallest company in the regiment suffered4 killed and several wounded. Sergeant Jeremiah Boyle, Private John Hurley and Corp James Cassidy were all killed at the wall by bullets to the chest. Cassidy carried a catholic prayer book in his breast pocket and the bullet that killed him penetrated the prayer book from a close range gunshot. Sergeant David Shane took a bullet in the left hand at the wall and Private Daniel Miles received several wounds, could not be moved, and died in November 9 in a Gettysburg Hospital. Privates Dolan and Mellon received minor wounds in the fight.

Corporal James Cassidy—Co H

Meanwhile in the center of the regiment the pressure mounted as the rebel line pressed up against and sometimes over the wall. "A fellow was taken in with me and I knocked him over and took him prisoner and took him in over the stone wall." (Author note—Years later at a Gettysburg reunion Robert Whittick would again meet this man, Sergeant Andrew B Willingham of Company A, Fifty-third Virginia and be recognized by the man he had captured. The Virginian said: "I knew him the minute I saw him . . ." **90** Then part of our regiment, company K, company G—parts of company G, I think it was, and D I think and C, were all together there, and company H, all in this mob while this shooting was going on. Some of them had their muskets reversed clubbing one another . . . . This is where our men commenced clubbing. There was too short range to fire at them." **91** Among the Confederates the casualties mounted. Col. James Hodges with the just arrived 14th Va. was riddled with bullets from the 69th line. **92** Beside him fell Major Robert Poore and Lieutenant Jenkins. Captain Richard Logan of Co H 14th Va. took a bullet in the heart as he approached the left of the 69th companies. Lieutenant John Neimeyer of Co I, 9th Va. took a bullet in the head as he neared the center of the 69th wall. It was later discovered that in front of that wall would lie the bodies of 727 rebels who died from the artillery or the rifles of the 69th Pennsylvania Volunteers. Just as Armistead's arrival stimulated the final push on the 69th front, his two left regiments the, 38th and 57th triggered another crossing of the wall with Armistead in the lead, his hat on his sword. Along with the remnants of the Garnett brigade about 150 men would leap the wall where the four companies of the 71st and companies I & A once stood. This final push began with confidence as the 72nd had pulled back behind the crest to reorganize and it looked as if the path was clear. This new wave also added to the rebels who pressed against the "refused right" of the 69th

The confidence of the 150 or so men with Armistead was temporary however as they saw that to their front the 72nd had reemerged at the crest; to their left the 71st and the 14th Connecticut were firing into their ranks and that to their right new troops of the 19th and 42nd Mass were firing from the rear of the trees. Armistead himself would get as far as the abandoned #3 gun of Cushing halfway up the slope from the wall.

Suddenly the men who were there with the 69th remember a turn in the fight. Different men described it in different ways. To some degree an understanding of the end of the fight requires that each memory be put into the context of perspective. Where was each observer on the battleground?

Banes in his book, *History of the Philadelphia Brigade,* writes from the perspective of a man who was somewhere in the rear of the 71st Pa at the top of the crest and amid the right companies of the 72nd Pa, "And now is the moment when the battle rages most furiously. Armistead, with a hundred and fifty of his Virginians, is inside our lines, only a few paces from our Brigade commander, they look each other in the face (sic). The artillery of the enemy ceases to fire, and the gunners of their batteries are plainly seen standing on their caissons to view the result, hoping for success. while Pettigrew's Division, following to support Picket, halts as if terrified at the scene. This is the soldier's part of the fight; tactics and alignments are thrown to one side. No effort is made to preserve a formation. Union men are intermingled with the enemy, and in some cases surrounded by them, but refusing to surrender. Rifles, bayonets and clubbed muskets are freely used and men on both sides rapidly fall. This struggle lasts but a few moments, when the enemy in the front throw down their arms, and, rushing through the lines of the Seventy-second, hasten to the rear as prisoners without a guard; while others who may have escaped, unwilling to risk a retreat by the path which they came, surrender" **93**. Major Roberts commanding the 72nd Pa recalled how his unit assembled at the crest of the hill. "The color guard was composed of Serg R Finecy, Corporals Brown, Steptoe, Giberson O' Donnell, Kaufman William Murphy. Serg Finecy fell with a half dozen balls in him, all the guard with the exception of Murphy, were killed or wounded, after the staff had been severed a few inches below where the colors are attached. Murphy seized the remaining portion and waving his cap advanced the colors to the fence. I was in command of the regt shortly afterward and promoted Murphy sergt—he was shot through the breast at Spotsylvania and died about six months later. Since Co E was the color company; it was on the left of Co F on the right. A was the extreme left and I on the extreme right of the regt—after the shelling on 3rd July when the regiment moved by the flank. I was on the right of the regiment with Company I. I recollect passing you, at the time you had a man by the collar who had run back from the battery, we passed so rapidly I could not catch fully the import of your remarks or his answer, beyond there were no men to work the battery. *I supposed the objective point of our movement to be the north fence* and so company I moved to within a few paces of the wall when the regt was brought to the front by someone on the left and I was compelled to dress company I to the left on the regiment by which time so many had injured by the fire that the right looked like as skirmish line"—**94**

Anthony McDermott, who stood at the top of the crest with the left companies of the 72nd Pa closer to Webb, consistently told of a battle which ended abruptly at the wounding of the two remaining rebel brigade commanders Armistead and Kemper, "The fighting here (at the wall to the left) continued until Gen. Kemper fell, seriously wounded near our colors; his men kept repeatedly calling upon our men to surrender . . . with Kemper's fall they surrendered . . . . We poured fire upon the enemy until Armistead received his mortal wound; he swerved from the way in which he, as though he was struck in the stomach, after wincing or bending like a person with cramp, he pressed his left hand on his stomach, his sword and hat (a slouch) fell to the ground. He then made two or three staggering steps, reached out his hands trying to grasp at the muzzle of what was then the 1st piece of Cushing's battery, and fell. At the time he was struck his fall was much about the time that Kemper fell . . . . His men threw down their arms, most of them lay down between us and the wall, to which we now returned. We sent all that surrendered to our rear, unarmed and leaving two troops behind to take charge of them." **95** In another recollection McDermott states "When Armistead fell, his men faltered and in a very few minutes they gave up, that is some threw themselves upon the ground while others ran back to the wall . . . . It was at this stage that Hall's Brigade came to behind the clump of trees and commenced firing" **96** Sergeant Joseph Garrett was to the south of Armistead over by the copse of trees and he remembered the end of the battle in his testimony at the Trial of the 72nd Pa.

Q—"What took place ?
A—as we were firing on the enemy Armistead fell
Q—Where did he fall?
A—He almost reached the gun before he fell
Q—What gun was that?
A—One of Cushing's guns
Q—Was it moved forward of its regular position?
A—Yes sir, I think it was
Q—Did you notice any other gun being moved down toward the wall?
A—Only the two in our company
Q—Where were they?
A—They were right at the wall: firing over the wall as the enemy approached
Q—Which of these guns was where you say Armistead fell?
A—The one left on the field

Q—How far up from the stone wall?

A—About forty paces

Q—When Armistead fell what took place?

A—It seemed that the fight ceased immediately afterwards

Q—When Armistead fell was there any surrendering?

A—Yes, sir

Q—What was being done with the rebels as they came in?

A—They were forced back to the rear as prisoners of war

Q—Was there any firing after Armistead fell?

A—I did not notice any

Q—State whether or not the fight was then over?

A—It was suppose to be over." 97

Private Hugh McKeever who was in the center of the 69th line still at the wall was also asked about the end of the fight . . .

Q—"Immediately after the fight did you see any rebels in the woods?

A—They were going to our rear as prisoners.

Q—Who took them prisoners?

A—We pushed them right back through our line

Q—As you took them you send them back to the woods?

A—No sir. We sent them into the right or left of the clump of trees, as you might call it.

Q—Did you know that Union troops were in the clump of trees?

A—No sir, not at the time. I learned afterwards.

Q—What troops were they?

A—They were Massachusetts troops." 98

McDermott in all of his writings insisted that when Armistead fell the fighting stopped, "The fighting stopped at that place. The fight may have been kept up a little longer on the left of our regiment" 99

The accounts of McDermott, Garnett, McKeever as well as Devereux and his adjutant William Hall all agree that the position of the Union forces at the time of the ending of the struggle was as follows from North to South: The 71st at the rear wall and touching the 72nd Pa which was at the crest. The 19th & 20th Massachusetts coming from south to north behind the copse of trees. The 42nd New York entering the copse of trees and the Sixty-ninth Pa stretched in a half circle its right against the northern edge of the copse of trees, its center a few yards behind the wall and it's left two companies bent southward at the edge of the copse. McDermott in his writings always gave credit to the men of Hall's Brigade for providing the psychological image of reinforcements rushing to the scene, which broke the spirit of the rebels who had crossed the wall. "The 69th has never claimed that no other troops came to their assistance, for we always allow that Hall's Brigade came up and were followed by the 72nd Pa." **100**

Once the fighting was over, the men of the 69th seemed to have a completely different focus than all of the troops now arriving down at the wall. These lads of the 69th had been in midst of all the fighting and they were focused on their comrades wounded, dead and dying. Not on gathering souvenirs and battle flags Many, including Private McKeever saw Colonel O'Kane before he died, "I saw Colonel O'Kane and he was then alive, but I went down to Taneytown road and he died afterwards." **101**

Down the slopes of the hill came the men from the 71st and the 72nd and from Massachusetts and New York. "None of the three regiments mentioned (72nd Pa 19th Mass and 42nd NY) fought in the "angle'. The nearest approach to it was the 72nd when they came to the crest of the ridge while Hall's men came in behind the clump of trees, almost to the crest of the ridge. Their coming up to our assistance was on a line diagonal to our position from our left and rear, not direct as your letter states, and if they mingled with our men it must have been on our left, certainly not on the right, while the fight was in progress." **102**

A private in the 72nd remembered this dash to the wall. "We then made a dash for them and on the way down I had the occasion to help a stranger, I suppose he was a member of the Sixty-ninth. He was about to bayonet a rebel who didn't have any arms and I stopped a moment and stopped him from doing that, and when I looked down our regiment was at the wall. That was within ten or fifteen yards of it." . . ." on my way down I saw them using the butts of their muskets, and by the time I got there the rebs had thrown down their arms and surrendered as prisoners, except a few that undertook to get back."**103** The behavior of the 72nd Pa years later would become a court battle but almost all the men of the 69th recalled only that the 72nd stayed on the crest of the ridge until the fighting was nearly over. Statements by those who were nearest to the fight made that clear. Lieutenant Michael Fay (Co D), Lieutenant William McNamara (Co I), Captain Patrick Tinen (Co D) and Corporal Patrick Moran all said that the 72nd never came closer than the top of the hill during the fight.**104**

Soldiers from the 71st Pa, 72nd Pa, 82nd NY, 19th Mass, 1st Minn., and even the 59th NY gathered up flags on the battlefield while the men of the 69th cared for their wounded and dead. Many of the men in the 69th returned to the wall immediately because they knew their comrades still lay on the ground beside it. McDermott wanted to know the fate of his tent mate, Thomas Diver. John Harvey wanted to care for his wounded son. Men from company F who had been fortunate enough to escape capture wanted to see who else was still alive at the wall. In his October 21st, 1889 letter to Bachelder, McDermott summed up the ending of the fight and the taking of the flags this way, "No flags were captured until the fighting had ceased. When the two companies (I&A) of the 69th who changed position were returning to the wall, the ground in addition to being covered with the dead and wounded of both sides, was thickly doted with rebels who had thrown themselves down and as we advanced back to the wall, these men surrendered, and we would send them to the rear and the troops behind of course seized them. The men of course were unarmed while the officers had their swords. That is the way Captain Reynolds of the 42nd NY captured his rebel Lieut. again. A large rebel flag stood up against the wall about where the 1st Co of the 69th stood (my company) I had gotten within abut 6 or 8 feet of it but was ordering rebels back to the rear as prisoners, when a soldier ran past me seized the flag and ran back. I suppose to his regiment. I spoke to him at the time making some remark belittling his act. I saw the figures 42 on his cap. I could have had that flag without any trouble, and if I thought acts like that would have brought a medal, its more than likely I would have preferred the flag to the gathering of prisoners. In a similar way the other flags were gathered up. That was the only man of the 42nfd NY or of any other regiment outside of our brigade that I saw at the wall. I have questioned our men of every company of the regiment from right to left and begged them to be truthful in their statements and tell me—did any other regiment go to the wall to assist us in repulsing Pickett. They all answered solemnly No !. This was at our last meeting on last Sunday afternoon. Most of the men say that there were individuals who came over the ground immediately afar the fighting ceased and it was these men who gathered up the flags." **105**

Another man, with Hall's Brigade, remembered the firing between rebels at the wall and his regiment behind the trees, "The enemy was safely layer down behind the wall, having planted their flags in the stones and poured a deadly fire into us from behind it, while our shots affected them little more than to prevent their advance further. We stood their fire perhaps five minutes, possibly more and lost fearfully . . . ." **106** Captain William Hall, adjutant of the `19th Massachusetts summed up quite nicely the ending of the combat. "The fighting, of course, ceased, as soon as those men threw down their arms and came in. Then there appeared to be a lull in the battle our men went down to about the angle where the 69th were at all events, only I suppose to see the 69th . . . . There was no fighting at this point after the enemy came in. The few who retired to get back across the filed ere not followed up and there was no fire, except an occasional shot. There was no organized fire, I mean. The men who went down there immediately after seemed to be prompted more by a sense of curiosity than through any need of their presence there . . . ." **107**

As soon as the fighting ended the musicians and members of the hospital detail of the 69th moved up to the wall and witnessed the carnage all up and down the line. There were men who needed medical care immediately. Colonel O'Kane was taken to the 2nd Corps Hospital, as was Major Duffy. John Harvey Jr. was taken to the Frey Barn, as was his first Sergeant Ralph Rickaby with his wound in the neck. The barn was soon filled with the wounded and dying, over 80 men. Outside, in yard, beside the barn, graves were being dug for the 30 already dead. All night, friends and comrades came down to the Red Barn along Taneytown road to spend a few minutes with men that they had lived with and fought with for two years. The regimental kitchens were prepared on the slope behind the crest of Cemetery Ridge. Adjutant Whildey had a slight arm wound that was bandaged so he could return to record keeping.

In front of the wall lay hundreds of rebels dead and dying. As darkness obscured the fields in front, the groans and cries of the dying could not be obscured from the ears of the men of the 69th Pa "Irish Volunteers".

After the battle the brigade reported to have captured a total of nearly one thousand prisoners and six battle flags. The men of the Philadelphia Brigade picked up 1400 rifles and muskets as well as nine hundred sets of accoutrements.

Across the fields in the Confederate camps, hundreds of wounded and dying filled the air with the sounds of post-battle. In the midst of these defeated rebels sat 16 men of the 69th Pa who had been captured during the attack and taken back to Seminary Ridge. They along with 10 men of the 71st pa and several other captured skirmishers from the Second Corps had little knowledge as to what awaited them in the morning.

General Webb would issue a subdued report 8 days later that would continue to reveal his attitude about the Irish 69th. He would factually report that "The Sixth-ninth Pennsylvania Volunteers lost all their field officers, but held its ground. The cover in its front was not well built, and it lost many men lying on the ground; still I saw none retire from the fence." In contrast, he reported on the action of the 106th Pa (which was 100 or more yards to the rear) stating "I lost gallant officers and men" and then went on to single out by name various brigade officers for conspicuous bravery. Not a man in the 69th was mentioned by name. **108**

Only years later would Webb give any real credit to the role played by the 69th. On Nov. 25, 1869 Webb wrote Bachelder "Having been shown by you my official report of the Battle of Gettysburg and having been asked to state whether or not I had any corrections to make in it . . . To do justice to the 69th Penn. Vols. and to the 71st that were with the 69th, I should have stated, that, leaving the 72nd Penn. Vols. in position I went to the 69th Regiment and formed them at the stone-wall and pointed out to them that a portion of the enemy was in their rear." **109**

On the evening of July 3rd, rations for three days were issued, and about midnight a heavy storm occurred, completely drenching the men and reducing the contents of their haversacks to a mass of pulp." **110**

CHAPTER SIX

PURSUIT OF LEE

The morning of July 4th dawned gloomy and wet and foggy. The rain had stopped sometime during the night but started again around 6:00AM. "The morning found many of the troops without food and no immediate prospect of obtaining any. Matters were rendered still worse from the fact that the condition of the dead about us required immediate attention. Burial parties were organized by the brigade, and several hundred bodies of the Confederate dad were placed in trenches to our front. Many of those engaged in this sad duty were well-nigh exhausted from hunger and fatigue" 1 Most of the work of the burial detail fell to the men of the 69th who had been detached to hospital and ambulance service plus men of the band. In addition, a number of men from the ranks offered their services. The ambulances and some wagons were driven through the gap in the fence to the left of the company G position and then down on the fields. Wounded men who had lain on the field for 16 hours or more were still being found and placed in ambulances. Piles of bodies were thrown on wagons and driven down toward the Emmittsburg Road for trench burial. All the time, pickets were kept out in the fields beyond the road to watch for rebel movements. There was fear of another attack, but no real danger existed because the Confederate were in retreat. That night the exhausted men of "the 69th Irish Volunteers" quickly fell asleep again by the wall they had defended with their lives . . . . *Their Wall.*

One of the unusual happenings after the Gettysburg battle ended occurred on the morning of July 5th. It seems that Private Farrell McGovern of company A had been taken prisoner on the skirmish line out by the Emmittsburg Road as the Confederates advanced during Picket's Charge. He was taken to the holding pens that were created behind the rebel lines and apparently, late in the evening of July 4, he signed parole papers and early in the morning was released to return to the union lines. Somehow as he worked his way toward the Union position he was shot and killed by a Confederate skirmisher. After the battle his body was recovered and he was returned home for burial. On July 10th a notice would appear in the Philadelphia Public Ledger: MCGOVERN—Shot by the rebels, near Gettysburg, on the morning of the 5th inst., as he was returning to our lines, after being paroled. FARRELL J. MCGOVERN, of Co. A, 69th Reg't. Penna Vols. aged 21 years. Due notice of the funeral will be given." On the afternoon of July 5th, the Sixty-Ninth left their position at the wall and marched down the Taneytown road to the east. Lee's Army was in full retreat and the Second Corps would attempt to circle ahead of Lee by marching east then south toward Hagerstown, Maryland. The unit needed to rest and reorganize before chasing anybody. A 12 mile march brought them to the little hamlet of Two Taverns where they made camp and were told that they would be give another full days stop. That night they enjoyed a clear sky, food and most importantly clean fresh air, free from the smells of decaying human flesh. Their wagon train was with them as was their commissary. Corporal Rittenhouse and his teamsters brought up all the tents, supplies and food to their campsite. That night they ate and slept in peace. Many in the regiment must have wondered who would take command of the 69th . . . . Captain Davis as senior Captain was in command but all the men knew that back in Philadelphia, Captain Thomas Kelly, whose brother had died with them at the wall, was ready to return to the regiment. He would receive orders to do so shortly.

In the evening of July 5th, Private James Dougherty from Company E slipped away from camp and began his return to Philadelphia to rejoin his wife and children. He would remain in Philadelphia until arrested November 24th, when he would be returned to the regiment and Court Martialed. The 21 year old Derry born blacksmith had been a model soldier since joining the 69th back in August 1861.

That evening 1st Lieutenant Charles McAnally sat down and wrote a letter to the wife of James Hand, his close friend, explaining her husbands death on July 3 . . . .

Camp of the 69th Regt P.V.

Near Gettysburg, Pa

July 5, 1863

Mrs. Jane Hand

It is a painful task for me to communicate the sad fate of your husband (my own Comrade) he was killed on the 3rd inst. He received a ball through the breast & one through the heart and never spoke after. I was in Command of the Skirmishers about one mile to the front & every inch of the ground was well contested until I reached our Regt. The Rebels made the attack in three lines of battle. As Soon as I reached our line, I met James. He ran & met me with a Canteen of water. I was near played. He said I was foolish didn't let them come at once. That the 69th was waiting for them. I threw off my coat and in 2 minutes we were at it—hand to hand they charged on us twice and we reputed them. They tried the Regt. on our Right and drove them which caused us to Swing back our right then we charged them on their left flank & in the charge James fell. May the Lord have mercy on his soul? He never flinched from his post and was loved by all that knew him. He is interned along side of Sergt. James McCabe, Sergt. Jeremiah Gallagher of our Company and 5 others of our Co. that you are not acquainted with. Our Co lost in killed, wounded and missing Twenty as follows Killed 8 Wounded 10 missing 2. Although we fought the Rebs 10 to one on the 2nd and killed or captured a whole Corps, our Co had only one man wounded that day the loss in the battle on the 3rd was heavy but all did not discourage the boys. We were determined that as long as a man lived he would stand to be killed too rather than have it Said that we lost on the battle field in Pennsylvania the laurels that we so dearly won in Strange States. The loss in the Regt. killed, wounded & missing was one Hundred and fifty eight. Our Colonel and Lieut. Col. and two captains Duffy and Thompson killed & Lieut. Kelly and 6 officers wounded. We killed 6 rebel generals and nearly all the line officers and killed or captured every man that attacked us in both days fighting. There never was a battle fought with more determination. In the first days fight the Rebels had our battery on the first Charge and we retook it again. Mrs. Hand please excuse this letter as I am Confused. I hope you will take your trouble with patience you know that God is merciful & good to his own. No one living this day was more attached than Jas & myself. When I was engaged in front, he wanted to get out to my assistance. I lost a loyal Comrade in him. No more at present from your sorrowing friend

Chas. McAnally
Lieut. Co. "D:" 69th
Regt P.V.

P.S. this letter will answer for Sergt McCabe. He was shot through the head. He died in 2 minutes after. McCabe had 25 cents of money $20 he lent to Lieut. Fay of our Co. We got no mail since the 19th until the rebs retreated last night. 2

Another letter was written that day by now Sergeant William C White of Company I who had participated in the entire Gettysburg fight . . . .

On the Battlefield near Gettysburg Pa July 5th 1863

I suppose you are worried about not hearing from me sooner. I had no time to write. We were marching every day since I wrote. We had two of the bloodiest battles ever fought. Our regiment was behind a stone wall. On the 2nd of July the rebels marched out on us and drove the men in front of us back and then marched to our stone wall. We fought them over an hour and then they turned and flew in all directions. In that days fight Captain Duffy and two of our men were killed.

On the 3rd they opened fire on our stone wall with over one hundred pieces of artillery. The shot and shell flew thick and fast. Tom Divvers was killed by a piece of shell. After they shelled us for about two hours they marched out in line of battle and charged on our stone wall and drove us from it about 50 yards. Then we turned and drove them back. I will write a full account after we get settled. The rebs have skedaddled. Ritchie, Cloney, and A. McDermott are safe.

Sgt. William C White, Co I, 69th P.V. 3

Meanwhile Major James Duffy's brother back in Philadelphia was already involved in writing to Governor Curtin about his brother future on July 7th . . . .

My Dear Sir,   July 7th 1863

My Brother Major James Duffy was wounded last Friday near Gettysburg. Drs. Pancost and son extracted a minie ball from his leg this morning. He begged of me to write you. He hopes to be able to take command in a few weeks his Col. was killed at his side- Col. Kane as was Lieutenant Col. Thudy. He being Senior officer of his regiment 69th Penna he hopes you will remember him for Col. position. Thank You so much but he is in hopes to be in the field in a few weeks and trusts you will kindly remember him

Your obt Sevt
Charles Duffy 4

Meanwhile back in Philadelphia former 1st Lieutenant Michael Cassidy died at his home from the bladder inflection that had plagued him since Antietam. After the incident concerning picket duty and the subsequent court martial, Cassidy returned to Philadelphia still ill and was cared for at his home from June 27th until his death. After his death his Wife Elizabeth filed for pension support and was turned down due to the court-martial verdict. It would takes 5 years and an eventual act of Congress to obtain a pension for his widow. During this fight the alignment of officers within the 69th again showed itself by the signatures of those who supported Mrs. Cassidy's 1868 pension appeals which asserted her husband's performance had been misjudged and involved prejudice . . . .

The undersigned, late officers of the 69th Regiment Penna Volunteers, having a personal knowledge that the within facts are true. Heartily concur in the petition of Mrs. Elizabeth Cassidy. Lieut. Cassidy was a faithful and diligent soldier, always with the exception herein referred to, prompt and willing to perform all the duties required of him.

Wm. Davis, late Col. 69th P.V.
F.F. Burmeister late surgeon 69th P.V.
James Duffy, late Major 69th P.V.
Joshua Owen, late Brig Gen.

Patrick Tinen, late Major of 69th P.V.
Eneas Dougherty, late 1st Lieut. 69th P.V.
Edward Thompson, late 1st Lieut. 69th P.V. 5

One can not help but note the irony that O'Kane, Tschudy, Whildey, Kelly and McNeil (The men who participated in the prosecution) had all died during the war at Gettysburg, Spotsylvania, Cold Harbor and Petersburg)

July 6th was a day of rest and began with a muster call to see what was left of "Paddy's Owen's Regulars". Captain William Davis of Company K was the senior captain and in charge of the regiment. He and Adjutant Whildey made up the entire Field Staff. All of the hospital staff had been left behind in Gettysburg to care for the sick and wounded. Several of these staffers would desert from the hospitals themselves over the next two months. In Camp Company A was commanded by Captain John McHugh and had 13 men present for duty. 2nd Lieutenant Murdock Campbell commanded Company B with 24 men. 1st Lieutenant Edward Fitzgerald had 18 men fit for duty with Company C. Captain Patrick Tinen was down to 18 from what was before Gettysburg the largest company in the regiment with 44 men. Company E stood with 19 under 2nd Lieutenant Devlin. The hard hit company F showed 11 present with Sergeant Gregg in command. Less than were now marching south as Prisoners of War. 15 men were prepared for duty with 1st Lieutenant Sherry in Company G, while the same number reported for duty in Company H under 1st lieutenant Thompson. In company I, 17 men were present to be led by 1st lieutenant McNamara. Finally 22 men were present and ready for duty with Company K now commanded by 1st Lieutenant Jack, a total of 174 officers and men in the 69th Pa. Several of these would get sick or desert in the next several weeks. after Gettysburg.

The acting commander of Company C, 2nd Lieutenant Charles Fitzpatrick had still not been mustered into the 1st Lieutenant position even thought he had been given the brevet post. He made his dissatisfaction very clear within the regiment and this helped for further strain his relationships with both Captain Davis and Brigadier General Webb. On July 7th he took out legal papers in the courthouse of Jefferson County Maryland to asset his right to be mustered as 1st Lieutenant. He received his commission papers on July 6th but was still not mustered. His unhappiness with the system finally would spill over when he decided to resign from the regiment the following month.

In the afternoon of July 6th after the roll had been taken Private Patrick Harvey, from company F, became the first post battle desertion from the 69th. Like many others who would desert over the next month, he had fought bravely at the wall but could stand the fighting no longer. His company had been almost overrun at the wall by the 28th Virginia and many of his friends were now prisoners being marched south with Lee's retreating army. Meanwhile back in Gettysburg Private James McNulty from company B died at the Division hospital at age 27.

The 69th had been sent by themselves to Two Taverns to regroup and rest. The rest of the brigade, the records show were sent directly to Taneytown and rested there. On the morning of July 7th at 5:00 am the 69th formed up and began a march to Taneytown to rejoin the brigade. On the road that morning John Cronin (Company 7) and Private Patrick Conniff (Company D) both deserted. Both men had fought at the wall at Gettysburg. When the 69th arrived at Taneytown they learned that the new Division commander, Brigadier General Alexander Hayes (John Gibbon had been wounded) had had some problems with Capt James Gleason, the Brigade Quartermaster. Gleason, of course, was the former Quartermaster of the 69th before Owen elevated him to brigade level. It seems that some disagreements about the placement and pace of the wagons had occurred.

Back in Gettysburg Michael Mullen from company G died in the Division hospital. Out on the battlefield citizens were beginning to arrive to seek the bodies of their loved ones killed in the struggle. Private Andrew McGuckin's (Co.B) brother arrived on the battlefield from Phoenixville to find his body . . . .

July 7, 1863

"I visited the battlefield after this battle with a number of others from Chester County Pa on Tuesday after the battle and I was viewing this cemetery of the dead killed in that battle and I noticed a board with the name of Andrew McGuckin name on it at the head of a newly made grave and I remarked to someone in my company that there lay one of our Phoenixville boys. Returning from the scene, I met Patrick McGuckin with a coffin. He was a brother of Andrew McGuckin. I asked him where he was going and he informed me after his brother Andrew. I told him I knew where he lay and I returned with him and he and I unearthed the remains of Andrew McGuckin found his shroud, an army blanket. I assisted to take him out of the grave and put him in the coffin and his brother Patrick McGuckin brought his remains back to Phoenixville." 6

Early on July 8th the regiment began a march south for 20 miles toward Frederick. They passed through the small towns of Bruceville, Pine Creek and Woodsboro. Finally they halted beside the Monocacy River at a hamlet called Walkersville. Many of the men used the opportunity to bath for the first time in many days in the river there. On July 9th, they arose and by 5:00 AM were on the road again marching toward the town of Frederick Maryland. By 8:00 they reached town and found themselves in a festive parade through the middle of the city. Hundreds of citizens had turned out, bands were playing, flags were flying and a festive atmosphere had taken over the town. The parade of the 2nd Corps was a spirited one indeed.

While the regiment paraded in Frederick, back home in Philadelphia the funeral of Colonel Dennis O'Kane was taking place. Colonel Dennis O'Kane's funeral was recorded in the *Catholic Herald Visitor* of 18 July 1863 . . .

"The funeral of Col. Dennis O'Kane, of the 69th regiment, who fell at Gettysburg, took place on Thursday morning, 9th inst., from his late residence, No. 575 Florida street. It was attended by many officers of the First Division P.V. and a large concourse of friends, preceded by Beck's Brass Band. The following named officers officiated as pallbearers:- General John D. Miles, Colonels W.D. Lewis and Turner G. Morehead; Lieutenant Colonel James Harvey; Captains Furey, Holbrook, Moran, Dillon, Rodgers, McCuen and Doyle; Lieutenants Ashe, Taggert, Dougherty, Woods, and McIlwayne. The funeral cortege was directed by Mr. Simon Gartland, undertaker, and slowly moved to St. James Church, West Philadelphia, where a High Mass was celebrated, and an appropriate discourse subsequently delivered by the pastor, Rev. Michael F. Martin. The service was solemnly sung by the choir. Miss Ashe presiding at the organ and at the OFFERTORIUM. A solo was sung by Mr. Harkins of St. John's choir, entitled "ECCE! DEUS SALVATOR MEU□ The interment took place in the Cathedral cemetery. 7

The funeral took place at the old St James church West Philadelphia from which O'Kane he was buried. Note: Florida St. is now named South Marvine St. It is possible that St. James church was chosen for the funeral Mass because the Rev. Michael F. Martin had been recently appointed to that church and

had already known O'Kane well from his service with the 69th during the
Peninsular campaign.

The 69th marched through Frederick from North to South and passed
through the hamlets of Jefferson and then Burkittsville (near Jeffersonville).
There they rested for two hours and then turned west marching through
Crampton's Gap in the South Mountain ridge. Finally, after a hard day the
Brigade rested at Rohrersville and made camp for the night. Along the way
Private John Eckard, age 25, in company A, deserted as they crossed South
Mountain. This would be his second desertion of the war after having been
given amnesty back in March 1863. His Sergeant, Stephen Dooley reported
"On the march after we left Gettysburg, we halted about two hours to rest
and stacked arms. When we started he (Eckard) and another man were
missing. He left his gun and that was the last we saw of him. I think it was
near Jeffersonville, Md." **8** Eckard would be captured, arrested and Court
Martialed by October 9th and returned to company A.

The next morning at 5:00AM, the 69th was off again through Locust
Grove, Reedsville and Smoketown. Many of the men all remembered the path
they had taken on these very same roads to Antietam back in September 1862.
As the men of the 69th passed by the Upper Bridge across the Antietam creek,
several noted that they had time to stop by the new cemetery in Sharpsburg
and to visit the graves of the men of the 69th still buried there. Seven men
from the 69th Pa had been laid to rest in the Sharpsburg Cemetery. The
final resting places had been marked and the lads of the 69th could pay their
respects. Three men from company C, Privates Michael Reedy, James Moss,
and Hugh McDevitt were buried there. From company G were Captain
Francis Bierworth and Private Bernard Carr. Private Beverly Vaugh was there
from company E and finally John Hand from Company K.

After a brief stop to honor their dead comrades the regiment marched on
down the Hagerstown Turnpike to the town of Tilghmantown after having
put 12 miles behind them since they awoke in Rohrersville that morning.
The next morning they would be on their way to where Lee's Army appeared
to be making a stand. Some two miles in the early morning of July 11th took
them to Jones Crossroads on the Hagerstown-Sharpsburg turnpike where
they moved across the fields and began entrenching. Then their orders were
changed, and they were off again toward Hagerstown. When they reached the
campus of Saint James College they moved toward the rebel entrenchments
and began digging their own earthworks. During this move forward at St
James College, Private William Watson in company A deserted the regiment
and was never seen again.

For the next 48 hours the 69th prepared for a frontal assault on the Confederate trench lines. They prepared their works; they rested and prepared their weapons. The word was passed that the attack would finally begin at 7:00AM on the 14th of July. Many wondered why Meade had allowed the rebs a full day to prepare for the assault when all the troops were in place on the morning of the 13th. The evening of July 13th saw the right five companies move forward in a drizzling rain. Companies I,A,F,D and H were led forward by Captain Tinen to a position to be ready for an attack. As morning approached the drizzle turned to a heavy rain. The soil of the Williamsport and Hagerstown area was softer than the soil of Gettysburg allowing the men to dig formidable trenches. Two men choose this time to desert the regiment. In company C Privates Thomas Lundy and William Farrell deserted. Lundy would be caught by Confederate partisans and end up wounded in a gun battle between the Confederate and a Union cavalry unit that rescued him, losing fingers on one hand. William Farrell, who had some personal problems with his company's officers and non-coms ended up returning to Philadelphia and joining the U.S. Marines for the remainder of the war. In fact he ended up serving in the Marines until about 1868.

As dawn rose on the 14th, the men of the 69th prepared for an attack. Then, pickets saw in the early light that lee's Army was gone. Over night they had slipped across the Potomac River and were safe in Virginia. Ahead of them had gone the men from the 69th who had been taken prisoners on July 3.

Meanwhile, in Virginia the 17 men of the 69th Pa who had been taken prisoner during the battle were herded southward toward Staunton, Virginia where the railroad to Richmond would take them to prison. The reader will recall that one of the prisoners was Private Patrick Anderson from Company D, who was captured while trying to join his regiment. Anderson may well have been mixed in with the soldiers of the first and twelfth corps and never joined in with the men taken on July 3. His tale of captivity is distinct from the remainder of the 17. At least one prisoner was already dead. Corporal Farrell McGovern seems to have been paroled as the rebels retreated and was killed by a Confederate picket as he made his way back to the union lines in the dark. The other 16 men were either taken while out on Picket line (probably Co D Privates Owen Clark, James Donohue and James Elliot) (The records show that Clark was probably wounded as well.) or were captured with Company F behind the wall.

These men were stripped of their haversacks and shoes and had their pockets searched for any valuables. They were forced to survive on the most meager of food along the march. All of them survived the 100 mile march to Staunton and were placed on railroad cars headed east to Richmond. When they arrived in Richmond they were inspected and determined to be either healthy or unhealthy. If they were healthy they would remain in prison until exchanged. If they were sick, they usually were given faster parole. We know that Owen Clark (Co. D) was wounded as were Privates Peter Smith (F) and Patrick Rafferty. We know that Private Patrick Leister (Co. F) was sick. We also know that Sergeant George Mulholland was sick as was Sergeant Robert Doake.

The two captured officers from Company F 1st Lieutenant John Ryan and 2nd Lt John Eagen were housed in Libby prison and would both be exchanged. 1st Lieutenant John Ryan would take sick with dysentery between August 11 and August 17 in the Libby Prison and be hospitalized. He would be paroled on March 7th. 2nd Lieutenant John Eagan would also be sick in the Libby hospital with an infection (which imply that he had suffered a slight wound at the Wall). He would be hospitalized from September 3 to September 20th and be paroled the same day as Ryan, March 7th. Unlike Ryan he would return to the company at Spotsylvania.

At least three men from the 69th were sick by the time they reached Richmond. Sergeant Robert Doake and Private Patrick Leister were sick and were paroled. Private James Hand got sick was hospitalized and then died on September 23, 1863

Four men from Company F died in Richmond prison before they could be exchanged. Private John McKinney died there Nov 20, 1863, wounded Private Patrick Rafferty on October 15, 1863 and Private Peter Smith just prior to the shift of prisoners to Andersonville, February 7, 1864. Two close friends, Corporal Arthur McLaughlin and Private Michael Gorman were captured with company F andwere at Belle Isle prison in December. Gorman later testified about the fate of Corporal McLaughlin . . . "one day they were called out to be counted and said McLaughlin, being very weak from want of food, staggered and the Rebel Officer struck him in the head with a stick he had in his hand, knocking him into a ditch and causing blood to flow from his mouth, nose and eyes; that his comrades picked him up and took care of him as well as they could; that he was unable afterwards to exert himself and his feet and legs and hands became frozen and he became so weak that deponent with some others took him up in a blanket and carried him outside the rebel works and placed him to be taken to the hospital. The surgeon who examined him stated he could not live and deponent never saw him alive afterwards and fully believes that he died a day or two afterward; that the date he was taken to the hospital was a few days after Christmas 1863." (Widow

Pension file of Arthur McLaughlin, testimony of Michael Gorman, National Archives Washington DC)

The healthiest and physically fit of the men remained in Richmond (usually at Belle Isle prison) until Andersonville Prison was completed in February 1864. Train to that camp would then transfer them. From Company D Privates James Donohue and James Elliot would be sent to Andersonville and die there. Elliot exactly one year after arriving at the Gettysburg Wall . . . . July 2, 1864 and Donohue on December 21, 1864. One man from Company F, Sergeant John O'Neill was shipped to Andersonville and died there June 13, 1864. Arthur McLaughlin's friend, Michael Gorman, remained at Belle Isle in Richmond and was not shipped to Andersonville. He would be paroled to City Point, Va. on March 15, 1864 then sent to Camp Parole Maryland and then given a furlough to return home. His three years with the 69th was over.

Private Patrick Liester from company D had been captured on the skirmish line along Emmittsburg Road during Pickett's Charge and would spend the next two months in captivity. He was able to write his wife after his parole and his letter gives the reader a graphic description of the conditions of the men of the 69th who were captured and marched south

Patrick Lester (Pvt. Co. F 69th Pa)
August 31, 1863 letter to wife
After Parole from Confederate Prison

Parole Camp Anoplus August 31 1863
My Deer wife and Children I take this opportunity of writing those few lines to you hoping to find you and the children in good health. I am in verry poor health My Self but I am as well as I can esspect after the treatment I got thuis last two Months Since I was taking prisener. We got only two ounses of bread to live on dayly and that the worst Fact we had to March 8 days one 18 ounces of flour Dear wife I can't tell you what we Suffered I hadebt a halfcent but what they tuck away. I hadnt a Shirt or Shoe or Stocking on the Jenie I was taking but I would not Stand it sow long but thinking of you and the children Dear wife I would not get of sow Soon only I was Sick. I am the only one that got paroled out the ridgement Dear wife you herd of all that was kiled out of the ridgement our Company was taking on the 3 days fight the Captain and Col was kiled before we war taking.

Wright as Soon as you possibly Can and Send Me a writing pen and Sone or to Strong Needles Deer wife we got new close when we landed heer thre ar plenty to eat but I cant eat it My Stomach is to weak Dear wife we got Mustered in today for to monts pay I expect we will be paid in a week or two. Wright as Soon as you Can Direct Your letter to Patrick Lester Collage green barracks anapolis Maryland Company F 69th PV. I will let you now more in my next letter. No more at present but remain your affectionate husband

Patrick Lester

Dear wife Send Me a little Money if you can but I now tiss hard for you to do but I Wasent ever Sow bad in the want of it.

As it became clear that the Confederate Army had successfully crossed the Potomac General Meade moved the Army of the Potomac into a defensive position. The 69th Pa was shifted to Falling Waters downstream along the Potomac River. That evening (July 14th) a whiskey ration was distributed to the regiment and the 69th slept beside the river. That night also two more men deserted from the regiment. **Private James Dolan and Private Edward O'Brien** from the same company left camp and disappeared. The two men had been friends during the war and it is logical to assume that they talked about and planned together their departure. Back in Phoenixville, Pennsylvania the body of private Andrew McGluckin had arrived home and been laid to rest at Saint Mary's Cemetery. The notice regarding his funeral, had appeared in the local newspaper . . . .

McGUCKIN—from wounds received at the battle near Gettysburg—July 3, 1863 ANDREW McGUCKIN, Co B 69th Regiment P.V.

The relatives and friends of this family are Respectfully invited to attend his funeral from the residence of his mother, Phoenixville Chester County, pa on Tuesday July 14th, 1863 at 10 o'clock." **9**

The next morning the march began again toward Sandy Hook and Harper's Ferry. The regiment traveled on a warm humid day through the hamlets of Downsville, Bakerfield and Sharpsburg and then made camp after covering 19 miles only two miles from Sandy Hook, Maryland.

On July 15, back in Philadelphia 24 year old company H private John Cassidy died at his home from his Gettysburg wounds. The bullet that pierced his prayer book and drove into his chest had ended his life after 22 days of struggle. His funeral notice was published in the Philadelphia Public Ledger the next day.

> "Mortally Wounded at the Battle of Gettysburg, JOHN CASIDY of Co H 69th Regiment P.V. in the 24th year of his age.
> The relatives and friends of the family are respectfully invited to attend the funeral, from the residence of his brother, William Cassidy N.W. Corner of Fifteenth and Wood Streets on Friday morning at 9 o'clock, without further notice. To proceed to Cathedral Cemetery. Funeral Service at Cathedral Chapel." **10**

On the same day July 15th, a funeral took place in Philadelphia for John Boyle of Company I who had written the short letters to his mother. His funeral notice appeared that day in thre Philadelphia Public Ledger . . . .

BOYLE—Killed at the battle of Gettysburg on the 3rd inst. Whilst nobly fighting for his country, JOHN F BOYLE OF Co. I 69th P.V. son of Catherine and the late Bernard Boyle, in the 22nd year of his age.
The relatives and friends of the family are invited to attend his funeral, from the residence of his mother, No 4 Walnut Place, Walnut St. below fourth, this Wednesday afternoon at 1 o'clock. Interment at St. Mary's Cemetery #557 **11**

Plans were not yet decided regarding the crossing of the Potomac River and so for two days the brigade camped at Pleasant Valley, Maryland. During this period, two more veterans of the Gettysburg campaign deserted. Corporal John Flood who was detached to the hospital as a cook deserted from his position back in Gettysburg, while Private John Harvey who had lost his son at the wall left camp and would be found a few months later without rifle or leathers dying in Washington DC from alcohol poison. The death of his son on July 3, it seems, killed his will to fight and his will to live.

The desertion of Private John Harvey Sr. would bring the number of men active on duty wit the regiment down to 158 men (9 officers and 149 enlisted soldiers) **12**

With the movement of command to Captain Thomas Kelly, the politics concerning Regimental leadership began. Captain William Davis had taken command at the death of Colonel O'Kane and with Lieutenant Colonel Martin Tschudy dead, and Major James Duffy severely wounded it was clear that a number of new positions would be filled in the regiment. Army regulations required that new officers would be appointed based upon the numbers of men reporting for active duty in the regiment. The severe losses at Gettysburg had driven the numbers of active duty soldiers within the 69th Penna Volunteers far below acceptable levels and thus it was not clear that a Colonel or even a Lieut. Colonel would be appointed anytime soon. In addition since James Duffy, recovering back in Philadelphia held the Major position; it might be some time before any promotions would be given.

Captain Davis and Captain Kelly were the two most logical candidates for command. Both were strong Irish Nationalists, although Kelly had been active with Irish militia groups and was much better known for his Irish militia leadership. Davis, on the other hand, had been active with the unit during the entire past year, unlike Kelly who had suffered a wound at Antietam resulting in two months recovery and then had been appointed by O'Kane as acting Quarter Master. Kelly had been with O'Kane in the original 24th Pa but Davis was by 1863 clearly closer to O'Kane and Tschudy. Time would prove that Kelly was the clear choice of the officers of the regiment.

EPILOGUE

After their remarkable steadfastness of the 69th at the wall in Gettysburg while their flanking regiments fell back, it was indeed ironic that not one man in the regiment would win the Congressional Medal of Honor. Those from other regiments, who picked up flags from those regiments shot to pieces by the 69th, received many honors. The 69th would regroup and go on to fight in The Overland Campaign. At The Wilderness, they fought on the Orange Plank Road. At Spotsylvania, they participated in the Mule Shoe attack on May 12th, capturing the flag of the 51st Georgia in hand to hand combat. They attacked at Spotsylvania again on May 18th. At Cold Harbor they assaulted the south end of the rebel lines. When the three year enlistment term expired for the men of the Philadelphia Brigade in the summer of 1864, only the soldiers of the 69th obtained the necessary 50% plus reenlistment requirement to continue as a regiment in the war. The other regiments of the Brigade, the 71st, 72nd and 102nd, were disbanded. The renewal of the men of Paddy's Owen Regulars was over 70%. From June 1864 to April 1865 the "Irish Volunteers" fought with the Second Corps, Second Division, Third Brigade. They swept westward to Ream's Station, Hatcher's Run and White Oak Road. The regiment pursued Lee west to Appomattox Courthouse. Of the 1007 men who had left Philadelphia in September 1861 only 56 arrived at Appomattox Courthouse in April 1865. All the rest had been killed, wounded and discharged, died of illness, taken prisoner, discharged after three year or deserted.

After the war, the survivors of the regiment organized an association to install a monument on the Gettysburg battlefield. This monument would be among the first regimental monuments placed there and would be dedicated in a ceremony July 2-3, 1887 that included the very first reunion of both Union and Confederate veterans of that battle. This dedication and reunion was done in conjunction with the Philadelphia brigade Association.

As the men of the 69th Pennsylvania "Irish Volunteers" began to pass away, they would always proudly call themselves veterans of Paddy Owen's Regulars

ENDNOTES

Chapter One—Background

Chapter Two—the Road to Gettysburg

1   Charles Banes, *History of the Philadelphia Brigade*, (Philadelphia: J.B. Lippincott & Company, 1876, Page 170

2   Elliot Diary, US Military Wa College, Carlisle, Pa.

3   O'Kane to Curtin June 3,1863 (Governor Letter Collection, Pa State Museum, Harrisburg, Pa)

4   Thomas Kelly letter to Gov Curtin June 3, 1863, service file, Nat Ar Wash DC

5   General orders June 5, 1863, 69th PVI General Order Collection National Archives Wash DC

6   Brief history of the 69th Page 26

7   Military File, John Frazier, National Archives, Washington DC.

8   Medical report, Patrick Garvin, Fairfax Seminary Hospital)

9   Patrick Leister file, National Archives, Washington DC

10 John McHugh Service file, Nat Ar wash DC

11 Medical report James Devine, National Archives, Washington DC

12　Pension application letter, Frederick Burmeister, January 17, 1880

13　General Orders 191 Army of the Potomac

14　Samuel Hammond Service File, National Archives, Washington DC

15　Charles Banes, *History of the Philadelphia Brigade*, (Philadelphia: J.B. Lippincott & Company, 1876, Page 176

16　Wainwright, Diary of Battle, pp 228-229

17　Elwood Corson service file, National Archives wash DC

18　Charles Banes, *History of the Philadelphia Brigade*, (Philadelphia: J.B. Lippincott & Company, 1876, Page 179

19　Gettysburg Tales, Pa 96

20　Charles Banes, *History of the Philadelphia Brigade*, (Philadelphia: J.B. Lippincott & Company, 1876, Page 179

Chapter Three—July Two

1　(72nd Pa Vs Gettysburg Monument Commission, age 261)

2　Anthony McDermott, *A Brief History of the 69th Regiment Pennsylvania Veteran Volunteers*, Philadelphia: D.J. Gallagher & Co., page 28

3　Letter from McDermott to Batchelder June 2, 1886, *Bachelder Papers*, Gettysburg, Pa

4　**Charles Banes, *History of the Philadelphia Brigade*, (Philadelphia: J.B. Lippincott & Company, 1876, Page 181**

5　(Medical and Surgical History of the War of Rebellion Part One Surgical Volumne 1870, MCNICHOLS FILE).

6　**Anthony McDermott, *A Brief History of the 69th Regiment Pennsylvania Veteran Volunteers*, Philadelphia: D.J. Gallagher & Co., page 28**

7   (McDermott to Batchelder June 2, 1886 Vol. 3, pp. 191-2) *Bachelder Papers*, Gettysburg, Pa.

8   (Letter from John Buckley to Colonel Batchelder)

9   Anthony McDermott, *A Brief History of the 69th Regiment Pennsylvania Veteran Volunteers*, Philadelphia: D.J. Gallagher & Co., page 29

10 Anthony McDermott, *A Brief History of the 69th Regiment Pennsylvania Veteran Volunteers*, Philadelphia: D.J. Gallagher & Co., page 28

11 (Letter from John Buckley to Colonel Batchelder, *Batchelder Papers*, Gettysburg, Pa)

Chapter Four—The Muster Call

Chapter Five—July Third—The Attack

1   Testimony of Robert Whittick, *72nd Pa vs. The Gettysburg Monument Commission*, page 80-81

2   John Buckley to John B. Bachelder, undated (John Buckley letters) Gettysburg Military Park Library Archives.

3   Many historians have noted that the 69th Pa was armed with a surplus of rifles as the rebels approached the wall and was therefore able to direct a heavy fire upon the attacking confederates. These historians note that the extra rifles came as a result of the men of the 69th being able to go out onto the fields in front of their position and gather rifles discarded by Wright's Brigade in their charge on July 2nd. The traditional source of this occurrence is usually statements made in a letter from John Buckley (company K-69th Pa) to John Batchelder where he states ". . . almost every man had from two to five guns loaded that were not used until Pickett got within fifty yards of the wall" (John Buckley to John B Bachelder, (John Buckley to John B Bachelder, Oct 10, 1889)

In addition to the Buckley citation, we also have three separate statements from Richard Penn Smith, commander of the 71st pa, regarding extra rifles. On November 25, 1867 in a letter to Peter Rothermal publisher of the Pennsylvania Historical and Museum Commission collection, Smith states "having a large pile of loaded guns by our side." (Richard Penn Smith to Peter Rothermal,

November 25th, 1867, Robert Broke Collection, U.S. Army Military History Institute, Carlisle, Pa) In 1887 in a letter to the Gettysburg Compiler June 7, 1887 Smith states "I directed officers and men to take from a pile of muskets, collected by my regiment on the previous day, as many capped or loaded guns as they could carry, and the officers and men of that portion of the regiment went into position behind a stone wall with from three to a dozen loaded guns each . . . ." (Richard Penn Smith, "The Battle", Gettysburg Compiler June 7, 1887). In a letter to Issac Wister Smith claims he had "300 extra guns which lay on the field" (Robert Penn Smith to Issac Jones Wister, July 29, 1863, Library of Wistar Institute Collection, Philadelphia, Pa)

The question must be asked: How could there have been enough discarded rifle-muskets laying around the field to the East of Emittsburg Pike to provide some 500-700 rifles to the 69th Pa and an additional 600 or more to the 71st Pa. It seems that the story exaggerated the number of extra rifles that were available that day. A close look at the losses of Brigadier General Ambrose R Wright's shows a total of 184 men killed, 343 men wounded and 169 men missing for a total of about 700 men. Now knowing that some of the casualties occurred out in the fields west of the Emmittsburg Pike and knowing that some of the wounded likely returned with their arms, we can not explain more that 1,000 extra rifles gathered. (Bradley M. Gottfried, "Wright's Charge on Jul;y 2, 1863", Gettysburg Magazine 17, 70-82) Even if we include some of the rifles lost by the two Union regiments overrun by Wright (The 15th Massachusetts and the 82nd New York—with about 320 in killed, wounded and captured) My estimated of the available "extra" rifles is about 500 or which both the 69th and the 71st could have gathered several hundred each. This would give the men of the left companies of the 69th from two to three extra each and the men at the rear wall with the 71st several extra each.

4   Anthony McDermott to John B Bachelder Letter, June 2, 1886

5   Testimony of Joseph McKeever, *72nd Pa vs. The Gettysburg Monument Commission*, Page 259.

6   Anthony McDermott, *A Brief History of the 69th Regiment Pennsylvania Veteran Volunteers*, Philadelphia: D.J. Gallagher & Co., page 29

7   Charles Banes, *History of the Philadelphia Brigade*, (Philadelphia: J.B. Lippincott & Company, 1876, 187-188

8   Testimony of Robert Whittick, *72nd Pa vs. The Gettysburg Monument Commission*, page 266)

9   Anthony McDermott speech never given, property of descendants

10 Ibid

11—Charles Banes, *History of the Philadelphia Brigade*, (Philadelphia: J.B. Lippincott & Company, 1876, Page 189

12—Anthony McDermott Letter to John B. Bachelder, June 2, 1886

13—Letter to Mrs. James Hand July 5, 1863, John Hand Pension file, National Archives, Washington D.C.

14—Testimony of George Hansel *72nd Pa vs. The Gettysburg Monument Commission*, 51-53

15—Testimony of Anthony McDermott, *72nd Pa vs. The Gettysburg Monument Commission*, page 237

16 Testimony of James Lynch, *72nd Pa vs. The Gettysburg Monument Commission*, page 304

17 Death Notice, Phila Public Ledger July 10, 1863

18—Samuel P. Bates, *History of the Pennsylvania Volunteers 1861-1865* Harrisburg: B. Singerly. 1869-1871, p. 788

19 One of the unsettled tactical debates concerning Pickett's Charge is the issue of how many companies of the 71st Pa were stationed at the front wall when Garnett's regiments arrived. A survey of the classic works on the fighting at the wall show a wide variety of views concerning how many companies of the 71st were at the front wall. If we review the works of Tucker, Coddington, Stewart, Hartwig, Rollins, Priest, Gottfried, Wert, Hess and Sears, we have a wide variety of combinations ranging from 2 companies at the front wall and eight at the rear wall to the opposite: 2 at the rear wall and 8 at the front wall. Unfortunately the lastest two books by Hess and Sears do not take up the debate at all but

rather follow from the views of earlier works. There are three primary sources that have been used by historians in dealing with the issue. Four separate letters from Colonel Robert Penn Smith; the testimony of Sergeant Major William Stockton of the 71st Pa; and a letter from Private (later Adjutant) Anthony McDermott. All four of Smith's letters talk about "half" of the regiment being forward and "half" being back OR "The left wing" being forward and the "right wing" being back. The testimony of William Stockton states that when the regiment moved forward two companies of the 71st "stepped on the rear wall" and later that "two companies were at the rear of the angle". The third source Anthony McDermott demonstrates how the Smith and Stockton view can be reconciled by observing that the 71st moved forward and occupied the front wall *and* the east-west wall and the rear wall (with two at the rear wall) and then those at the east-west wall were pulled back to the rear. This McDermott view is also comfirmed by a careful reading of the comments regarding the original "echelon" placement of the companies of the 71st by Smith in his Compiler Article (Smith: Robert Penn Smith to Sister, July 17, 1863, Library of Wistar Institute Collection, Philadelphia, Pa; Robert Penn Smith to Issac Jones Wister, July 29, 1863, Library of Wistar Institute Collection, Philadelphia, Pa; Richard Penn Smith to Peter Rothermal, November 25th, 1867, Robert Broke Collection, U.S. Army Military History Institute, Carlisle, Pa, Richard Penn Smith, "The Battle", Gettysburg Compiler June 7, 1887.) (Testimony of William Stockton, *72nd Pa vs. The Gettysburg Monument Commission*, 242-250.) (Anthony McDermott to John B. Bachelder, October 21, 1899.)

My views on this issue are formed by an extensive examination of the compiled service files of all of the men of the 71st who were in the battle as well as all of the available pension records. I have extracted and analyzed the names and the numbers of 71st soldiers who were killed, wounded or captured on July 3rd. In addition, I have walked and measured the ground upon which the front companies of the regiment fought. My conclusion is consistent with the eyewitness views of Smith and Stocker and McDermott.

There are only 105 feet of available space for the placement of companies at the front wall by the 71st Pa. This allows for only four companies.

All of the men captured on July 3 belonged to companies K,G,H & C of the 71st. These are the four front companies.

The non-bombardment losses in killed and wounded of companies K, G.H & C (30) are almost double the number reported for the other 6 companies (17).

Gary Lash in his recent regimental history of the 71st Pennsylvania was kind enough to include my theory regarding the number of companies at the front wall in his footnote section. While he did not adopt my views, and holds to the traditional eight companies forward, he was fairly accurate when he stated that my theory is based upon "topographical and casualty" perspective. Actually my theory is based upon both "topographical and casualty (with special emphasis upon prisoners taken)" perspective. Lash correctly points out that the use of killed and wounded figures are problematic because we can not know if these figures occurred during the fight at the wall, during the flight from the wall or during the counterattack against the wall or for that matter during the bombardment. However the use of "taken prisoner" figures for July 3 are a clear indication of company location since the only captives from the 71st who could have been taken by the rebels would have to be from the front companies. These prisoners are mentioned by numerous Confederate accounts but until research was done their names and, more importantly, their companies were not known. As it turns out every single one of the 11 known prisoners taken that day were from four companies, C,H,G, & K. Their names were 1st Lt. Jacob Devine, Corporal Jesse Hill, Private John Perkins, Private James Kensalla, Private William Bradley, Private Steven Hafferty, Private Charles Kelly, Corporal Andrew Gallagher, Private James Nelson, Private Thomas Woods and Sergeant Major William Stockton.

Only next should we then survey the killed and wounded figures in the action we discover that the killed and wounded for these four companies are twice the level of all of the other 6 companies. Then we consider that the only two 71st soldiers who wrote after the war about being at the front wall when Garnett's regiments arrived were John Burns and John Beidleman from companies C & G.

Gary Lash is the first historian to give some of the names to the men of the 71st who were captured at Gettysburg. However, his list contains at least two mistakes, that if not mistaken, would throw doubt onto my listings of 71st prisoners taken. Lash lists Private Patrick Conner of company F, 71st Pa, as taken prisoners at the wall on July 3rd and Private Andrew Gallagher of Co G 71st as taken prisoner on Culp's Hill on July 2. In fact when we check the compiled service records of Connor, he is listed four separate times as having been taken prisoner on the night of July 2. The records of Gallagher are a little more confusing. On his prisoner of war card he is listed as having been taken on July 2, however on his compiled service files he is listed several times as having been captured July 3. When we check the morning muster records of his company (G) we find Gary G. Lash, *"Duty Well Done:" The History of Edward Baker's California Regiment*, (Baltimore: Butternut & Blue, 2001) 335-345.)that there is no Private missing on the morning of July 3rd.

It is my view that a though review of the first hand accounts and an analysis of the captured as well as killed wounded figures from the July 3rd action will result in a conclusion that four companies (K,G,H & C) were stationed at the front wall when the rebel troops under General Richard Garnett approached.

20—Testimony of Anthony McDermott, *72nd Pa vs. The Gettysburg Monument Commission*, page 220)

21—Letter from Anthony McDermott to John B. Bachelder June 2, 1886

22—Testimony of Joseph W. Garnett, *72nd Pa vs. The Gettysburg Monument Commission*, page *254*

23—Ibid, page *255*

24—Anthony McDermott, *A Brief History of the 69th Regiment Pennsylvania Veteran Volunteers*, Philadelphia: D.J. Gallagher & Co., page 31

25—Letter from Anthony McDermott to John B. Bachelder, Oct 21, 1899.

26—Samuel Roberts to Alexander S. Webb, August 18, 1888.

27—Charles Banes, *History of the Philadelphia Brigade*, (Philadelphia: J.B. Lippincott & Company, 1876, Page 190

28—Testimony of Joseph W Garnett, *72nd Pa vs. The Gettysburg Monument Commission*, page 251

29—Testimony of Hugh McKeever, *72nd Pa vs. The Gettysburg Monument Commission*, Page 259)

30—Berkeley to Daniel, September 26 _____, J.W. Daniel Papers, Box 23, University of Virginia Library. Charlottesville, Va.

31—Henry Owen, "Pickett's Charge", Gettysburg Compiler, (April 6, 1881), p.1

32 David Johnson, *Four Years a Soldier,* (Princeton WV, 1887) Page 234

33 William H. Taylor, "Some Experiences of a Confederate Assistant Surgeon", *Transactions of the College of Physicians of Philadelphia*, Vol 28, page 118.

34 Randolph Shotwell, "Virginia and North Carolina in the Battle of Gettysburg", Our Living and Our Dead IV (1876), page 93.

35—Anthony *McDermott to John B. Batchelder, June 2, 1886*

36 Testimony of Anthony McDermott, *72nd Pa vs. The Gettysburg Monument Commission*, page 220.

37 Anthony *McDermott to John B. Batchelder, June 2, 1886*

38 George W. Finley, "Bloody Angle", *Buffalo Evening News*, May 29 1894, P. 43

39 Compiled Service Records of 71st Pa, National Archives, Washington D.C.

40 George W. Finley, "Bloody Angle", *Buffalo Evening News*, May 29 1894, P. 43

41 Testimony of Private Thomas Reed, *72nd Pa vs. The Gettysburg Monument Commission*, page 56.

42 Testimony of Samuel Roberts, *72nd Pa vs. The Gettysburg Monument Commission*, page 150.

43 Testimony of Frederick Boland, *72nd Pa vs. The Gettysburg Monument Commission*, page 120.

44 Testimony of Charles Banes, *72nd Pa vs. The Gettysburg Monument Commission*, Page 282

45 Testimony of Joseph Garrett, *72nd Pa vs. The Gettysburg Monument Commission*, page 251-254

46 Testimony of Anthony McDermott, *72nd Pa vs. The Gettysburg Monument Commission*, page 220.

47 Anthony McDermott to John B. Bachelder June 2, 1886, p 5

48   Charles Banes, *History of the Philadelphia Brigade*, (Philadelphia: J.B. Lippincott & Company, 1876, Page 191

49   Testimony of Anthony McDermott, *72nd Pa vs. The Gettysburg Monument Commission*, page 220

50   Testimony of Anthony McDermott, *72nd Pa vs. The Gettysburg Monument Commission*, page 220

51   Testimony of Anthony McDermott, *72nd Pa vs. The Gettysburg Monument Commission*, page 223

52   Compiled Service Records of 71st Pa, National Archives, Washington D.C.

53   *Anthony McDermott to Bachelder letter June 2, 1886 page 5)*

54   Testimony of Hugh McKeever, *72nd Pa vs. The Gettysburg Monument Commission*, page 264

55   All taken from individual pension files at National Archives, Washington D.C.

56   The story of Company F of the 69th Pennsylvania Infantry is a little known episode in the midst of the widely studied assault on July 3, 1863. The fact that many of the soldiers in Company F were taken prisoner by men from Richard Garnett's rebel brigade was well recorded by the men of the 69th as soon as the battle ended. The testimony of men such as Joseph McKeever (p.263), and Anthony McDermott (p. 234) in the 72nd Pa vs. The Gettysburg Monument Commission. Most of what we know about the specifics comes from a letter from Anthony McDermott to John Bachelder dated June 2, 1886. The single Confederate reference is from Sergeant Drewry Easley (Company H, 14th Virginia) who makes it clear that the union prisoners were taken at the wall before Armistead's line reached that position. (D.B Easley, "With Armistead When he was killed", CV, 20 (August 1912), P. 379) Almost all historians from Coddington and Tucker to Hess and Sears mention the capture of men from company F in passing. For example Hess writes, "McDermott believed that they managed to grab only two men of the regiment, other than those members of company F who were gobbled up wholesale when Armistead's 100 men crossed the fence. There was some fierce hand to hand fighting at and near the position of Company F" (Earl J. Hess, *Pickett's Charge-The Last Attack at Gettysburg*,Chapel Hill: University of North

Carolina Press, Page 285) Stephen Sears writes, "Their rush forward impelled the command of the 69th Pennsylvania to order the three rightmost companies to swing back 90 degrees to counter the charge. Two companies did so, but the captain of the third was killed before he could give the order and nearly all his men were overrun and captured" (Stephen W. Sears, *Gettysburg* (Boston: Houghton Mifflin Co. Page 449)

The details of the capture of the men of company F are explained in this chapter. However one historian has advanced a description of the Company F action that widely differs from the traditional view and from my analysis.

In 1998 Michael Priest in his book *Into the Fight—Picketts' Charge at Gettysburg* presented his readers with a completely new version of the Company F story which added elements never seen before . . . . "Company F which was suppose to be the hinge of the formation, did not execute the command. When the Confederates killed Captain George Thompson before he had time to relay the command to his company, his lieutenants—John Ryan and John Eagan—sent their men over the wall into Confederates ranks. For a few seconds, they engaged the Rebels with bared muzzles and with rifle butts until the Rebels captured or wounded the entire company". Priest added to the scene several new elements. First, that Company F had crossed over the wall into rebel ranks, second that they had engaged in fighting the Confederates on the west side of the wall and third that this charge was ordered by the two lieutenants. (John M. Priest, *Into the Fight Pickett's Charge at Gettysburg* (Shippensberg: White Mane 1998), Page 127.)

After reading this version, I immediately turned to the footnote section and carefully examined the sources Priest had used for these new elements of the story of Company F. I discovered that after examination of all the footnote sources that none of the new elements in Priests version could be found. Nothing in the pension papers or the compiled service records of the two lieutenants supported this version. Nothing in the testimony of either McDermott or McKeever supported this version.

Upon further investigation I noticed that Priest had used a transcription of the letter from Anthony McDermott to Bachelder which is printed in the Bachelder Papers containing an important error in transcription. The original McDermott statement in his letter to Batchelder reads "Company F was completely hustled over the stone wall . . . ." (McDermott to Batchelder, June 2, 1886,Page 5) The transcription appearing in the Batchelder book reads "Company "F" completely hustled over the stone wall . . ." (Ladd & Ladd, The Bachelder Papers, III, p. 1411)

Perhaps the active verb "hustled" vs. the passive verb "was hustled" resulted in the notion that the men of company F leaped across the wall into hand to hand combat after being ordered to "charge" by the two lieutenants. No evidence exists for the new Priest version. In addition, a careful examination of the individual service records shows that in fact not all the men of company F at the wall were taken prisoner.

57   D.B. Easely, "With Armistead when he was killed", CV, 20 (August 1912), Page 379

58   "About the Death of General Garnett", Confederate Veteran Magazine, XIV (February 1905), page 81

59   Charles McAnally to Mrs. James Hand July 5, 1863.

60   Anthony McDermott to John B. Bachelder June 2, 1886.

61   Anthony McDermott, *A Brief History of the 69th Regiment Pennsylvania Veteran Volunteers*, Philadelphia: D.J. Gallagher & Co., page 31.

62—Charles McAnally to Mrs. James Hand, July 5, 1863.

63—(Letters in The North American and Philadelphian, May 4, 1904)

64   Anthony McDermott to John B Bachelder, June 6, 1886, page 6.

65—Testimony of Anthony McDermott, *72nd Pa vs. The Gettysburg Monument Commission*, page 222.

66—(Compiled testimony, The 72nd Pa Vs The Gettysburg Monument Commission, pp 171-172)

67   Anthony McDermott to John B. Batchelder, June 2,1886

68   Alfred Carpenter's Letter, (Company K, 1st Minnesota Volunteer Infantry Regiment), written July 30, 1863

69   Harry Abbott to his brother, July 7, 1863

70   Another one of the unsettled tactical debates that surrounds the Pickett's Charge event is the behavior and motions of the 72nd Pa regiment during the attack.

This debate is one that not only involves historians but also became a legal case in the Penna Supreme Court in 1889. In that year a controversy between the survivors of the 72nd Pa and the Gettysburg Monument Commission erupted over the proper location for the placement of the monument of the 72nd Pa on the Gettysburg Battlefield. The Gettysburg Monument Commission had decided to locate the 72nd monument along Hancock Avenue at the crest of the hill based upon their research that showed that the 72nd Pa was a reserve unit and that their battleline was located at that position. The rule that the commission had established for all regimental markers was to place the monument at the battleline location of each regiment and not at subsequent locations that the regiment may have moved as the battle progressed. The survivors of the 72nd Pa organization protested this location selection and argued that their monument should be located along the front wall where the "left wing" of the 71st Pa had been positioned at the start of the fighting. Their logic was that the 72nd charged to this location during the fighting. The case first went to the Adams County Court of Common Pleas in January 1889, which ruled in favor of the Monument Commission. The survivors of the 72nd then appealed the case to the Supreme Court of Penna in the summer of 1889 and got a reversal.

For historians of the event, the trial produced a 369-page gold mine of testimony from former officers and soldiers who witnessed the event. It also produced a mass of contradictory and confusing eyewitness accounts to the reader. The specific actions of the 72nd remain clouded but the basic pattern is as follows.

During the bombardment the 72nd Pa was stationed behind the crest of Cemetery Ridge directly behind the copse of trees and received a severe degree of fire. With most of the shells of the rebel artillery over firing the wall, many shells and projectiles landed amid the 72nd ranks. (72nd Pa vs. The Gettysburg Monument Commission) As the infantry assault began crossing the fields, the 72nd was ordered into battleline on the back of the crest directly behind the copse of trees. Once in line they were ordered by their commander, Major Samuel Roberts, to move in an oblique direction to the right which would bring them to a point abut 80 yards east of the front wall and directly at the crest of the hill opposite the section of the wall being abandoned by the four companies of the 71st Pa. (Testimony of William Good (p. 41); Charles Vessels (p.75); Henry Russell (p. 99); Elwood Hamilton (p.107); Rene Boerner (p. 116); Frederick Boland (p.121) etc, *72nd Pa vs. The Gettysburg Monument Commission*) As they moved to the oblique right, the rightmost company got ahead of the rest of the regiment and Major Roberts ran over to bring them back into line. This left the commander of the regiment off to the right of the regiment (testimony of Samuel Roberts, *72nd Pennsylvania vs the Gettysburg Monument Commission*, 149-150). As they arrived at this point, the confederates in the 56th and 28th Virginia had taken the front wall and were beginning to fire from behind it. The 72nd opened fire with a volley that killed and wounded some of the Confederates who had jumped the wall (testimony of Frederick Mannes (p.86); James Wilson (p.137); *72nd Pa vs. The Gettysburg Monument Commission*). For a short time, fire was exchanged between rebels protected by the wall and the 72nd at the crest in the open. Most of the killed and wounded from the 72nd fell at this point. (Testimony of Samuel Roberts (P. 150); Jesse Mews, (p.45); Thomas Read (p. 56);Frank Weible (p.69); Charles Vessels (p.75); Henry Russell (p.99); Elwood Hamilton (p.107); Frederick Boland (p.121); Robert McBride (p.125); James Johnston (p. 147);etc., *72nd Pennsylvania vs. The Gettysburg Monument Commission*)). It was also at his point that General Webb ran over to the color Sergeant of the 72nd and unsuccessfully ordered the regiment forward. Major Roberts was off on the right flank and was wounded. Some of the companies on the right pulled back on the backside of the crest to regroup. (testimony of Frederick Mannes, *72nd Pennsylvania vs. The Gettysburg Monument Commission*, page.86); (George W. Finley, "Bloody Angle", *Buffalo Evening News*, May 29 1894, page 43) and at that point Armistead and his men crossed the wall. The 72nd then moved forward again and volleyed into Armistead's men. At some undetermined point in time, the 72nd Pa began to move forward toward the wall. (testimony of Thomas Montgomery (p. 136); James Wilson (p.137); all other 72nd Pa witnesses; *72nd Pa vs. The Gettysburg Monument Commission*) The evidence is unclear as to how much time elapsed before this movement began. What is clear is that most (if not all) of the fighting had ended by the time the 72nd reached the wall position.

71   Testimony of James Lynch, *72nd Pa vs. The Gettysburg Monument Commission*, page 305

72   Another of the unsettled tactical issues in Pickett's Charge involves the behavior and movement of the 59th New York Infantry. This regiment made up of only four companies was posted as part of Hall's brigade directly to the left of the 69th Pa's company G. What action these four companies took during the approach of the confederate infantry on July 3rd has been a mystery which needs exploration. The problem is that no direct evidence exists regarding their actions during Pickett's Charge. All OR references to the regiment discuss their participation in the counterattack against rebel troops already at the wall. Historians have employed two different approaches to the issue of the 59th New York. Some have said nothing

about the unit and have simply shown them on a map along the wall before the fight began and most have used various circumstantial and indirect evidence to assert that the regiment retreated before the rebel onslaught on their position. At the dedication of their monument, four speakers presented talks on the regiment. Unfortunately, the focus of the talks was on the regiment's general civil war history and the role they played in the counterattack without any reference at all to the time period when the rebels reached the wall. In fact, three of the four speakers at the ceremony were not even with the regiment at Gettysburg.

The treatment of the 59th in the most recent of works treat the regiment as one which broke and retreated in the face of rebel attack to their front and Cowen's canister fire from their rear. For example Stephen Sears in his recent work writes "At about the same time, to the south, beyond the Copse, a second gap abruptly opened in the Federal line. This was at the position of the 59th New York, the rightmost regiment in Norman Hall's brigade. The 59th was in a bad way to begin with. By the time of Gettysburg it had been consolidated into just four companies, and in Thursday's fight it lost (among others) its commander, Lieutenant Colonel Max Thoman. Now, as Kemper's Virginians turned and came right toward it, the 59th suddenly and unaccountably bolted. Captain John H. Smith of the 11th Virginia remembered the moment: In the Yankee battle line directly in front of him he "could see first a few and then more and more and more—and presently to my surprise and delight, the whole line break away in flight." (Stephen Sears, *Gettysburg* (New York: Houghton Mifflin, 2003, page 445.) Earl Hess painted a similar picture in his recent work, "At this pressing stage of the advance a good number of the 59th New York gave way. Exactly why it happened was never explained; indeed, no one in the regiment even admitted it ever happened. The regiment was placed directly in front of Cowan, who reported that it "turned and broke." There is some indication that those who retreated were in the right wing. This forced the 7th Michigan to slightly refuse its left flank. Members of the 59th put the best face possible on this incident. Capt. William McFadden, who wrote the official report for the regiment, made no mention of any problems. "The behavior of both men and officers during the [attack] was excellent, ably sustaining the past reputation of the Third Brigade." Lt. Henry N. Hamilton went so far as to make the entirely fictitious claim that the 82nd New York and 7th Michigan, to left and right of the 59th, gave way under the pressure, "leaving our regiment to contend with them alone." (Earl Hess, *Pickett's Charge* (Chapel Hill: University of North Carolina Press) page 242.)

My own research into the issue focused on the examination of the compiled service records and pensions of all of the men of the 59th who were at the battle on July 2nd and July 3rd and into the history of the regiment prior to Gettysburg. When Sears says that the 59th was "in a bad way" he actually understates the leaderless and demoralized condition of the regiment.

Before the consolidation of the regiment into four companies, the regiment's colonel, William Northedge, had been court martialed and dismissed for inciting mutiny; conduct unbecoming and drunkenness. The Major, James Purdy, resigned due to a battle wound. The Lieutentant Colonel, Max Thoman was fatally wounded July 2nd and The Adjutant, William Pohlman would be wounded and leave the field during the bombardment. Three of the four company commanders were missing as the rebels approached. To state that the regiment lacked leadership is an understatement.

In addition, an examination of the casualties of the regiment during the pre-assault bombardment shows that the 59th was especially hard hit by confederate artillery fire. Unlike the regiments to their left and right who had stone wall and fence protection, the area occupied by the 59th was low and the middle of their line included a wagon opening in the short dirt mound that did exist. No fewer than 15 men were killed or wounded during the artillery bombardment. The day before the 59th had been hit head-on by Wright's assault with a loss of 15 men (including their commander Max Thoman).

Then, we must add the fact that Cowen's artillery battery with five guns was being set up directly behind the regiment, firing canister over their heads. According to the accounts of the 69th Pa to their right, rebels occupied the wall position precisely where the 59th had been stationed. According to Cowen, rebels charged his guns from the wall position precisely where the 59th had been stationed. According to at least three separate confederate accounts, soldiers in gray occupied the wall position precisely where the 59th had been stationed. (Berkeley to Daniel, 26 September, Daniel Papers University of Virginia; John Holmes Smith reminiscences, February 4-5, 1904, Daniel Papers, University of Virginia; Martin & Smith, "The Battle of Gettysburg, and the Charge of Picket's Division, page 193")

Finally to consider the idea that the 59th New York remained at the wall without leaders, under Cowen's canister fire and after severe bombardment losses requires a look at the regiment's losses after the bombardment ended. While the four right companies of the 69th (G,K,B,E) lost 45 men killed and wounded (37%-45 of 132) after the fighting ended, a complete review of the service and pension records of every man in the 59th New York present that day shows only 7 men killed or wounded . . . a mere 6% (8 of 140) between the end of the cannonade and the end of the fighting. We know that men of the 59th NY were involved in the counterattack at the end of the fight and logic compels us to feel that the eight causalities occurred at that time.

While no direct proof has yet been discovered regarding the location of the 59th New York during the assault, an examination of the leadership, organization, July 2 losses, bombardment losses and post-bombardment losses leads this writer to the conclusion that the 59th New York did not remain at the front wall when Picket's troops arrived there on July 3rd, 1863.

73 Testimony of John Buckley, *72nd Pa vs. The Gettysburg Monument Commission*, page 135.

74 Anthony McDermott, *A Brief History of the 69th Regiment Pennsylvania Veteran Volunteers*, Philadelphia: D.J. Gallagher & Co., page 32

75 Johnson, Four Years a Soldier, (page 263Princeton W.V. 1887)

76—Report of Capt. A.N. Jones, July 7 1863, George Edward Pickett Papers, Perkins Library, Duke University

77—Randolph Shotwell, "Virginia and North carolina in the battle of Gettuysburg, *Our Living and Our Dead IV*, page 93.

78—Testimony of John Buckley, *72nd Pa vs. The Gettysburg Monument Commission*, Page 135.

79—Testimony of Arthur Deveraux. *72nd Pa vs. The Gettysburg Monument Commission*, page 185.

80—Testimony of William Hall, *72nd Pa vs. The Gettysburg Monument Commission*, page 210.

81 John Buckley to John B Bachelder, Oct 10, 1889

82—John Buckley to John B. Batchelder, October 10, 1889

83—John Buckley to John B. Batchelder, October 10, 1889

84—John Buckley GAR remembrance form, Gettysburg National Park Library files, Gettysburg, Pa.

85—Major Peyton 19th Virginia. OR Series 1 Vol. 27 Part 2 pp. 385-387

86—Testimony of Robert Whittick, *72nd Pa vs. The Gettysburg Monument Commission*, pp. 80-81.

87—Robinson, *18th Virginia*, Page 21

88—Testimony of Hugh McKeever, *72nd Pa vs. The Gettysburg Monument Commission*, page 263.

89—Edmund Berkeley to Daniels, September 26 _____, Daniels Papers, University of Virginia, Charlotte, Va.

90—*Philadelphia Times*, July 3, 1887

91—Testimony of Robert Whittick, *72nd Pa vs. The Gettysburg Monument Commission*, pp. 81 &84.

92 (Theodore Gates, The Uster Guard and the War of Rebellion" (New York; B.H. Tyrell, 1879, p 415)

93—Charles Banes, *History of the Philadelphia Brigade*, (Philadelphia: J.B. Lippincott & Company, 1876, Page 191

94—Samuel Roberts to Alexander S. Webb, August 18, 1888.

95—Anthony McDermott to John B. Batchelder, June 2, 1886.

96—Anthony McDermott to John B. Batchelder, Sept 17, 1889.

97—Testimony of Joseph Garrett, *72nd Pa vs. The Gettysburg Monument Commission*, 251-252.

98—Testimony of Hugh McKeever, *72nd Pa vs. The Gettysburg Monument Commission*, page 265.

99—Testimony of Anthony McDermott, *72nd Pa vs. The Gettysburg Monument Commission*, page 223.

100—Anthony McDermott to John B. Bachelder, Oct 21, 1889.

101—Testimony of Hugh McKeever, *72nd Pa vs. The Gettysburg Monument Commission*, page 268.

102 (McDermott Letter to Batchelder Oct 10, 1889)

103—Testimony of Thomas Reed Co F, *72nd Pa vs. The Gettysburg Monument Commission*, page 56

104 102 (McDermott Letter to Batchelder Oct 10, 1889)

105—Anthony McDermott to John B. Bachelder, Oct 21, 1889.

106—A.C. Plaisted to John B. Bachelder, June 11, 1870.

107—Report of Norman J. Hall, *72nd Pa vs. The Gettysburg Monument Commission*,Page 210

108—(Webb Report, July 12, 1863, OR

109—Alexander Webb to John B Bachelder, Nov 25, 1869.

110—Charles Banes, *History of the Philadelphia Brigade*, (Philadelphia: J.B. Lippincott & Company, 1876, Page 191

Chapter Six—In Pursuit of Lee

1—Charles Banes, *History of the Philadelphia Brigade*, (Philadelphia: J.B. Lippincott & Company, 1876, Page 196

2—Charles McAnally to Mrs. James Hand, July 5, 1863.

3—(Letters of William C White, July 5, 1863, Private Collection)

4—Charles Duffy to Governor Curtion, July 7, 1863, Pa Archives, Harrisburg, Pa

5—Charles Cassidy pension file, national Archives Washington

6—(John Robarbs, McGuckin Pension file National Archives)

7—*Catholic Herald Visitor* of 18 July 1863 . . .

8—(Proceedings of John Eckard's Court Martial October 9, 1863)

9—(Philadelphia Public Ledger, July 8, 1863)

10—(Philadelphia Public Ledger 16 July, 1863)

11—(Philadelphia Public Ledger 16 July, 1863)

12—(July 31 Muster report, 69th PVI, National Archives)

For a full minute by minute regimental mapping of the assault
"Great Charge"
$12.95
749 Aldrin Ave, Lansdale, Pa 19446
www.Pa69irish.com/great_charge

PHOTO CREDITS

Cover—Battle of Gettysburg, Lithograph by L. Prang, 1887

US Library of Congress Collection